INTERNAL CONTROLS FOR COMPUTERIZED SYSTEMS

INTERNAL CONTROLS FOR COMPUTERIZED SYSTEMS

JERRY FITZGERALD

Edited and Designed
By
Susan V. Welling,
Palo Alto, California

PUBLISHED BY:

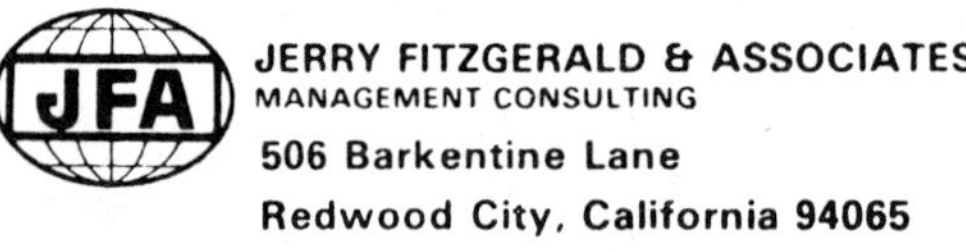

Printed in the United States of America
Library of Congress Catalog Card Number 78-69677
International Standard Book Number 0-932410-04-9

CONTENTS

FIGURES

ABOUT THE AUTHOR

Dr. Jerry FitzGerald is the principal in Jerry FitzGerald & Associates, a management consulting firm located in Redwood City, California. He has extensive experience in systems analysis, EDP auditing, data processing security, data communications/teleprocessing as well as in the development of seminars and training courses in the above disciplines.

As a consultant, Dr. FitzGerald has been active in numerous system design projects, EDP audit reviews, EDP security assurance reviews, in the development of functions such as computer security administrator and quality assurance organizations, and has interfaced with both data processing organizations and internal audit organizations with regard to auditing during the system development life cycle. Dr. FitzGerald has also been active in the review and validation of distributed versus centralized on-line systems and has worked on numerous data communications and telecommunications networks. He has taught EDP auditing, systems analysis, and data communication courses and seminars at the university level and to practitioners in the field. These courses and seminars have been conducted for both private industry and governmental agencies as well as for the University of California at Berkeley, California State Polytechnic University at Pomona and California State University, Hayward.

Dr. FitzGerald has been a tenured Associate Professor in the California University system, and a Senior Management Consultant at SRI International. His other professional experience includes positions as Senior System Designer for a computer manufacturer, a Systems Engineer for a major medical center, and a Programmer for an aerospace firm.

Dr. FitzGerald's educational background includes a Ph.D in business administration, an MBA, and a bachelor's degree in industrial engineering. He has written extensively; besides this book he has published *Fundamentals of Data Communications* and *Fundamentals of Systems Analysis* (both published by John Wiley & Sons, New York). His other publications include numerous articles, such as "Protecting Data Communication Networks," published by the Computer Security Institute (Supplement Computer Security No. 21; March/April 1978), and "Designing for Auditability," published by *Datamation* in August 1977. His 18 years of combined business, educational, and consulting experience have involved such organizations as banks, credit unions, governmental agencies, stockbrokers, electronic funds transfer (EFT) networks, computer manufacturers, certified public accountants, aerospace firms, health care/pharmaceutical firms, educational institutions, and management consulting organizations.

This book has specifically drawn on the author's expertise in systems analysis and EDP auditing. The controls presented here have been collected during years of consulting work. The author has also applied controls collected during his work on the System Auditability and Control (SAC) reports published during 1977 by the Institute of Internal Auditors (this project was funded by the International Business Machines Corporation). While at SRI International, Dr. FitzGerald was the principal consultant for this study.

PREFACE

Because of the explosive growth of on-line distributed systems, a new and more practical method of focusing the appropriate controls toward these on-line systems is required. This book contains over 650 controls and is organized into ten chapters—an explanatory introduction and nine chapters—which divide the data processing function into its basic components. Each of the nine chapters contains a matrix of controls that interrelates the organization's concerns/exposures with the specific resources/assets that must be reviewed. These chapters and accompanying matrices cover:

- General organizational controls (chapter 2)
- Input controls (chapter 3)
- Data communication controls (chapter 4)
- Program/computer processing controls (chapter 5)
- Output controls (chapter 6)
- On-line terminal/distributed systems controls (chapter 7)
- Physical security controls (chapter 8)
- Data base controls (chapter 9)
- System software controls (chapter 10)

The matrix approach subdivides a sophisticated data processing system into its specific components, such as the data communication network. Then the controls that relate to each component of the on-line system are reviewed.

This book can be used in numerous ways; the most prevalent one will be for designing new or enhancing current computerized systems, conducting internal control reviews, evaluating risk analysis, developing EDP audit plans, and developing organizational control standards.

The author would like to graciously acknowledge the assistance of Dr. Ray Roberts and Mr. Warren Stallings, Jr., for their efforts in reviewing this work, and especially Mr. Stallings for his assistance in the placement of specific controls within the cells of the control matrices.

Jerry FitzGerald

INTRODUCTION TO CONTROL MATRICES

This chapter explains how to utilize the control matrix approach and defines who might use this book, as well as the various uses of control matrices. After a thorough review of this chapter, the reader should be able to utilize the hundreds of controls contained in the nine matrices when designing or enhancing computerized systems, conducting internal control reviews, developing specific audit plans, conducting risk analyses, or developing standards.

THE NEED FOR CONTROLS

The management of an entity is responsible for establishing and maintaining adequate internal controls. The establishment and maintenance of a system of internal controls is a significant management obligation. A number of developments have triggered considerable increased interest in the subject of internal controls. Among these developments have been:

- Explosive growth in data processing technology.
- Wider use of data processing by organizations of all sizes, especially smaller organizations because of the growth in the use of minicomputers and microprocessors.
- Increased dependence upon on-line distributed data processing systems and the growing recognition of the impact data processing has on every facet of today's organization in providing accounting, production, and management-related information.
- Increased utilization of data communications (teleprocessing).
- Widely publicized cases of alleged computer fraud or breaches of privacy.
- Increased liability by directors and officers of organizations and the growing concern over the shift in control responsibilities and techniques that must be effected to maintain an adequate infrastructure of organizational controls.
- Increased attention expressed by the ever-growing number of audit committees at the director level.
- The emphasis by public accountants on internal control systems.

- The Foreign Corrupt Practices Act of 1977. *

To further emphasize the need for controls, it should be noted that in recent years, organizations have become increasingly dependent upon computer hardware, software, and data processing personnel. This commitment to computerization has changed the potential vulnerability of the organization's assets because the traditional security, audit, and control mechanisms take on a new and different form in a computer-based system.

A complex on-line data communication-oriented system consists of various combinations of hardware, software, facilities, people, and the policies and procedures that interrelate these components. The many diverse components and potential entry-points into a complex on-line system make it possible for a person with sufficient technical or applications knowledge to enter the system and make unauthorized manipulations of data, programs, or operational procedures. Furthermore, control procedures for an on-line system cut across many lines of responsibility within an organization, creating a control problem in itself. For instance, several departments within an organization may share in the exercise of the control procedures and each department may be responsible for only one segment of the overall control plan. The integration of controls among the various components of such a complex on-line system is the infrastructure upon which a secure on-line data communication-oriented system must be based.

This increased reliance upon computers, the consolidation of many previously manual operations onto computer systems, the shared responsibility between different departments for control procedures, and the fact that on-line systems cut across many lines of responsibility have increased management's concern about the adequacy of the present control mechanisms in use in the EDP environment.

While the use of computers is rising, it is also evident that a far greater potential exists to control errors and omissions, disastrous events, fraud, and other adverse occurrences in automated systems than in the manual systems that have been replaced. Finally, management's concern over adequate controls will be for naught if the data processing system designers, EDP auditors, and their managers do not have the proper training and control techniques to utilize when designing or reviewing the internal controls associated with on-line computerized systems.

WHO MIGHT USE THIS BOOK

This book is a working tool to be utilized by those personnel who are designated to carry out management's policies and procedures with regard to safeguarding the assets of the organization. It is meant to be a first-level working tool. It contains hundreds of specific controls that can be applied to the various components of the organization's computerized systems. The specific personnel who will find this book of value in conducting their day-to-day job responsibilities include the following:

- System designers and programmers who design new computerized systems and enhance current systems.

---

* Organizations should be aware of how the Foreign Corrupt Practices Act of 1977 changes the Securities and Exchange Act of 1934, particularly the following: "Reporting companies are also required to: Devise and maintain a system of internal accounting controls sufficient to provide reasonable assurances that— (a) Transactions are executed in accordance with management's general or specific authorization; (b) Transactions are recorded as necessary: (1) to permit preparation of financial statements in conformity with generally accepted accounting principles or any other criteria applicable to such statements; and (2) to maintain accountability for its assets; (c) Access to assets is permitted only in accordance with management's general or specific authorization; and (d) The recorded accountability for assets is compared with existing assets at reasonable intervals and appropriate action is taken with respect to any differences."

- EDP auditors who conduct internal control reviews, interface with data processing during the development of new systems, and perform all the other functions involved in EDP auditing (this includes both *internal auditors* and the organization's *public auditor*).

- Management personnel such as the management involved in data processing, those in the audit function, and the like.

- The computer security administrator who might be responsible for the security, privacy, and information control aspects of the organization.

- The quality assurance specialist who might be responsible for insuring the internal control aspects of the organization's computerized systems.
- The risk analysis manager who might be responsible for conducting risk analyses and various aspects of insurance.

- The operational personnel who are involved with the day-to-day operation of the data processing function as well as those operational personnel who are involved with other day-to-day business operations for the organization.

- Governmental regulatory agency personnel.

- Educators in data processing, auditing, and accounting.

USES OF THE CONTROL MATRICES

The nine matrices contained in this book are used to logically organize the hundreds of controls and to relate them to specific functional areas of data processing systems. Each control matrix is in a chapter by itself and can be used very effectively in carrying out the day-to-day job responsibilities with regard to:

- Designing new or enhancing current on-line computerized systems.

- Conducting an internal control review with regard to data processing-related systems.

- Evaluating and developing controls during a new system design review.

- Developing and evaluating the various safeguards with regard to a risk analysis plan.

- Conducting an EDP security assurance review.

- Developing specific EDP audit plans.

- Developing organizational standards for use when designing new computerized on-line/distributed systems.

- Developing an organizational EDP audit manual.

- Developing the general organizational controls and specific physical security controls for the data processing function.

- Familiarizing personnel with controls in a specific data processing functional area.

- Educating and training data processing and audit personnel.

The primary use of this book will be by data processing system designers and programmers when designing or enhancing systems and by EDP auditors (both internal auditors and public auditors) when conducting internal control reviews.

ORGANIZATION OF THIS BOOK

This book on internal controls for computerized systems is organized into ten chapters. It is very important that the reader thoroughly understand this first chapter, because it is here that we explain how to use the control matrices (the next section of this chapter explains how to use the control matrix approach). More than 650 practical controls are listed in this book. They are organized into nine individual control matrices (chapters 2 through 10), as follows:

- General organizational controls
- Input controls
- Data communication controls
- Program/computer processing controls
- Output controls
- On-line terminal/distributed systems controls
- Physical security controls
- Data base controls
- System software controls.

HOW TO USE THE CONTROL MATRIX APPROACH

In order to effectively utilize the control matrix review approach, the reader should become generally familiar with the overall data processing functions and the various components of each system such as the on-line terminals, the data communication network, and the data bases. Figure 1-1 identifies the nine components of a data processing system and it is for each of these components that there is a corresponding control matrix in chapters 2 through 10 of this book. For example, before utilizing a specific matrix, first determine which one of the nine components of the system is being reviewed. Are the on-line terminal controls being reviewed? The data communication controls? And so on. Then utilize the control matrix pertaining to that component to review the specific controls that might be applicable.

After choosing the appropriate control matrix, use it in conjunction with whatever internal control review methodology is used by the organization. In other words, the control matrices are a tool that will interrelate the several hundred controls described in this book to each of the nine components of a data processing system depicted in Figure 1-1.

The nine control matrices do not comprise a methodology on the conduct of an internal control review. Instead, the overall methodology on how to conduct an internal control review is assumed to be already established within the organization. The matrix approach of this book is a tool that works with the diverse methodologies for conducting internal control reviews that are in use by a variety of organizations.

To utilize the control matrices, look at the sample matrix in Figure 1-2 (this matrix was taken from chapter 4 and involves the review of the data communication network

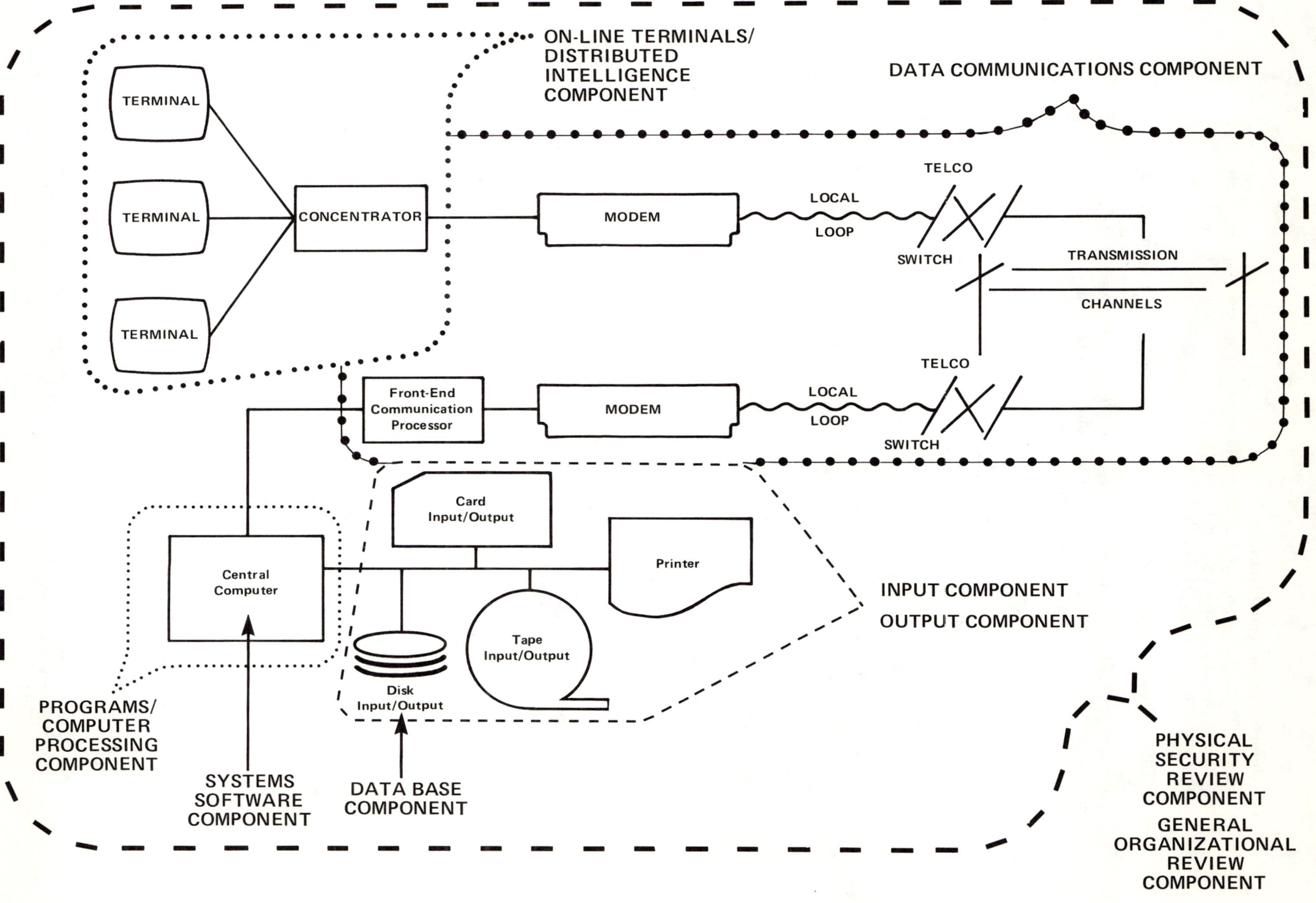

FIGURE 1-1: COMPONENTS OF A DATA PROCESSING SYSTEM

controls). The various concerns/exposures* to which a data communication network may be subjected are listed across the top of the matrix. The various resources/assets† that should be reviewed are listed on the left vertical axis of the matrix.

The concerns/exposures and the resources/assets change from chapter to chapter because each chapter's control matrix is involved with only one of the nine components of the data processing system. Also, for each chapter's matrix, each of the concerns/exposures and each of the resources/assets are individually defined to enable the reader to thoroughly understand each exposure and each asset.

In conducting the control review, any resource/asset (left vertical column) that might be subject to a concern/exposure (top horizontal row) should have some type of control/safeguard that must be evaluated and reviewed. These controls/safeguards are represented by the numbers within the cells of the matrix, which correspond to the list of controls in each chapter. Therefore, referring to Figure 1-2, if the concern/exposure was "message loss or change" and if the resource/asset being reviewed was "the front-end communication processor," then the appropriate controls that should be evaluated and reviewed are numerically listed at the intersecting cell of the matrix. There are numerous numbers listed in this cell. The specific controls that correspond to these numbers are defined within the chapter. Our example in Figure 1-2, extracted from chapter 4, highlights one of the controls (control 89) in order to exemplify the specific type of control to which we are referring.

As a further example of the versatility of the matrices in chapters 2 through 10, they may be utilized in any of four major approaches, as follows:

1. **THE RESOURCE/ASSET APPROACH**

   - Identify the appropriate resource/asset on the left vertical axis of the matrix. This would correspond to a physical asset or some other identifiable function or procedure that was being reviewed.
   - Read across the row identifying each potential concern/exposure to which the resource/asset may be subjected.
   - Evaluate and review each potential control/safeguard (these are listed by number within the cells of the matrix) for its applicability with respect to protecting the resource/asset from each concern/exposure.

2. **THE CONCERN/EXPOSURE APPROACH**

   - Identify the appropriate concern/exposure along the top row of the matrix. This would correspond to the specific concern or exposure that was being reviewed.
   - Read down the column identifying each resource/asset upon which this concern/exposure has an effect.
   - Evaluate and review each potential control/safeguard (these are listed by number within the cells of the matrix) for its applicability with respect to protecting each resource/asset from the concern/exposure.

---

* A *concern/exposure* is defined as a potential threat area or an adverse occurrence that could be injurious to the organization.

† A *resource/asset* is defined as the item that is being reviewed, such as computer hardware, software programs, operational policies or procedures, personnel, and other tangible or intangible assets.

CONCERNS / EXPOSURES

RESOURCES / ASSETS

	ERRORS AND OMISSIONS	MESSAGE LOSS OR CHANGE	DISASTERS AND DISRUPTIONS	PRIVACY	SECURITY/ THEFT	RELIABILITY (UP-TIME)	RECOVERY AND RESTART	ERROR HANDLING	DATA VALIDATION & CHECKING				
CENTRAL SYSTEM	1-4, 39, 41-43 47, 48	1-5, [illegible] 37, 39 48, [illegible] 89	1, 8, 11, [illegible] 40, 48, 50 51, [illegible] 58 64, 65, [illegible]	6, 8, 24, 35, 53 [illegible] 62, 68 70, 72-74, 77-80	6, 8, 24, 35, 53 56, 60, [illegible] 72-74, 77-80	1, 13, 16, 29, [illegible] 63-65, 68, 81, 88	50, 51, 63-65	48, 85, 89	6, 24, [illegible] 47, [illegible]				
SOFTWARE	1-4, 39, 41-43 46-49, 52	1-5, [illegible] 37, 39 41, [illegible] 48, 49 52, [illegible] 89	[illegible]	[illegible]	[illegible]	[illegible]	50-52, 61, 63 64, 68	48, 61, 85, 89	[illegible] 47 [illegible] 55				
FRONT-END COMMUNICATION PROCESSOR	1-4, 34, 39 41-44, 46-48	1-5, 7, 34, 37 39, 41, 42, 49 89	1, 8, [illegible] 40, 44, 48, [illegible] 51, 54, 57, 58, 64, 65, 79, 85	[illegible] 62, 68 70, 72-74, 78-80	35, 37, 39, [illegible] 60, 62, 68, 70 72-74, 78-80	[illegible] 30, 34, 36, 40 43, 44, 50, 51 63-65, 81, 88	37, 50, 51 63-65	43, 48, 85, 89	6, 24, 39, 45, 47, 48, 38				
MULTIPLEXER, CONCENTRATOR SWITCH	1-4, 7, [illegible] 41, 44, 46, 47	1-5, 7, 37, 39 [illegible]	1, 8, 13, 16, 29, [illegible] 33, 40, 44, 48, [illegible] 54, 57, 58, 65, 79, 85	6, 8, 24, 35, 37 45, 60, 62, 68 [illegible] 78-80	6, 8, 24, 29, 35, 37, 39, 45, 60, 62, 68, 70, [illegible] 74, 78-80	1, 13, 16, 29, 30, 32-34, 36, 40, 44, 50, 51 [illegible]	37, 50, 51, [illegible] 64		[illegible] 41 45, 47, 48, [illegible]				
COMMUNICATION CIRCUITS (LINES)	12, 2[illegible]	28, 70, 91	10, 15, 16, 18, [illegible]	25, 28, 68, 70 [illegible]	25, 28, 68, [illegible] 75, 76, 78 91	[illegible]							
LOCAL LOOP	12	[illegible]	[illegible]	[illegible]	[illegible] 75, 7[illegible]		[illegible]						
MODEMS	12, 18	[illegible]	[illegible]	[illegible]		9-11, 13-18, 21 23, 36, 88	9-11, 14, 15, 63, 64	18-20, 22, 23					
PEOPLE	5, 39	[illegible]	[illegible]	[illegible]	[illegible] 24, 29 [illegible] 71, 74, [illegible] 80	81, 82, 85-87	50, 51, 86, 87	49, 86, 87, 89, 90	6, 88				
TERMINALS/ DISTRIBUTED INTELLIGENCE	[illegible]	[illegible]	[illegible]	[illegible]	[illegible] 29, [illegible] 3, 56, 62, 70	1, 40, 88	63, 64		6, 24, 45				

SEE CHAPTER 7 FOR MOST OF THESE CONTROLS

DEFINITION OF A CONCERN/EXPOSURE

THE LOSS OF MESSAGES AS THEY ARE TRANSMITTED THROUGHOUT THE DATA COMMUNICATION SYSTEM OR THE ACCIDENTAL/INTENTIONAL CHANGING OF MESSAGES DURING TRANSMISSION.

ALL THE CONTROLS LISTED DOWN THIS COLUMN ARE THOSE THAT CAN BE UTILIZED TO SAFEGUARD AGAINST A "MESSAGE LOSS OR CHANGE."

EXAMPLE OF A SPECIFIC CONTROL FROM THE LIST GIVEN IN THIS CHAPTER

89. REVIEW ERROR RECORDING TO REDUCE LOST MESSAGES. ALL ERRORS IN TRANSMISSION OF MESSAGES IN THE SYSTEM SHOULD BE LOGGED AND THIS LOG SHOULD INCLUDE THE TYPE OF ERROR, THE TIME AND DATE, THE TERMINAL, THE CIRCUIT, THE TERMINAL OPERATOR, AND THE NUMBER OF TIMES THE MESSAGE WAS RETRANSMITTED BEFORE IT WAS CORRECTLY RECEIVED.

ALL THE CONTROLS LISTED ACROSS THIS ROW ARE THOSE THAT CAN BE UTILIZED TO SAFEGUARD THE "FRONT-END COMMUNICATION PROCESSOR."

DEFINITION OF A RESOURCE/ASSET

A HARDWARE DEVICE THAT INTERCONNECTS ALL THE DATA COMMUNICATION CIRCUITS (LINES) TO THE CENTRAL COMPUTER OR DISTRIBUTED COMPUTERS AND PERFORMS A SUBSET OF THE FOLLOWING FUNCTIONS: CODE AND SPEED CONVERSION, PROTOCOL, ERROR DETECTION AND CORRECTION, FORMAT CHECKING, AUTHENTICATION, DATA VALIDATION, STATISTICAL DATA GATHERING, POLLING/ADDRESSING, INSERTION/DELETION OF LINE CONTROL CODES, AND THE LIKE.

FIGURE 1-2: SAMPLE MATRIX ON DATA COMMUNICATIONS

3. **ALL CONTROLS FOR A RESOURCE/ASSET**

- Identify the specific resource/asset that requires some controls/safeguards.

- Read across the row copying the numbers (disregard duplicates) for the controls/safeguards. In this way *all* the controls that relate to a specific resource or asset will be covered.

- Evaluate and review each potential control/safeguard for its applicability with respect to protecting the resource/asset.

4. **ALL CONTROLS FOR A CONCERN/EXPOSURE**

- Identify the specific concern/exposure that requires some controls/safeguards.

- Read down the column copying the numbers (disregard duplicates) for the controls/safeguards. In this way *all* the controls that relate to a specific concern or exposure will be covered.

- Evaluate and review each potential control/safeguard for its applicability with respect to mitigating the effects of the concern or exposure.

Each control matrix is presented in a separate chapter. Within each chapter, all the resources/assets that will be reviewed are defined, as are all the concerns/exposures. Following these definitions is a numerical listing of all the controls/safeguards that are applicable to that specific control matrix (component of a data processing system). Each chapter, then, will have its own unique matrix containing its own specific resources/assets, its own specific concerns/exposures, and its own unique list of controls/safeguards that should be evaluated and reviewed. Overall, there are in excess of 650 controls in this book.

GENERAL ORGANIZATIONAL CONTROL MATRIX

This chapter defines and discusses the general organizational controls that are applicable to an organization (private industry or government). This internal control review matrix is to be used when reviewing the general controls that affect administrative control, accounting control policies, organizational structures, and the like. Internal controls in an organization include controls that may be characterized as either administrative or accounting; therefore, this control matrix can be used when reviewing an entire organization or some of its departments and especially the data processing functions.

THE MATRIX APPROACH

The internal control area to be reviewed using this matrix covers the general organizational controls that overlay an entire organization and its specific internal departments. These controls involve the highest levels of management and pass on down through the entire organization to the daily operational levels. When reviewing the general organizational controls, match each resource/asset with its corresponding concern/exposure as listed in Figure 2-1: General Organizational Control Matrix. This matrix lists the resources in relation to the potential exposures and cross-relates these with the various controls/safeguards that should be considered when reviewing the general organizational controls (see chapter 1 for an explanation of how to use the control matrix approach).

Immediately following the matrix is a definition of each of the concerns/exposures that are listed across the top of the matrix and each of the resources/assets that are listed down the left vertical column of the matrix. Following these definitions is a complete numerical listing and description of each of the controls/safeguards that are listed numerically in the cells of the matrix.

CONCERNS/EXPOSURES

The following concerns/exposures are those that are directly applicable to the general organizational controls that should be in place within the organization. The definition for each of these exposures, listed across the top of the matrix, is as follows:

- Management Control—The degree of control implemented by the management of the organization. In this case, the management of the organization is defined as including those top management officials at the highest levels of the company (president, audit committee, etc.) on down to the level of management that is responsible for the day-to-day implementation and use of the various management control procedures. The management control in the data processing area should be specifically reviewed with regard to the data processing systems.

- Management Reporting—The various reports that feed back to the different management levels of the organization. These may include scheduled reports, demand reports, and exception reports, and may include reporting down through the chain of command or back up through the management chain of command.

- Fraud/Defalcation—The safeguarding of the organization's assets (including informational assets) from their unauthorized removal either by persons trusted by the organization (employees, vendors, etc.) or by outsiders who are not directly related with the organization.

- Privacy—The accidental or intentional release of data about an individual, assuming that the release of this personal information was improper to the normal conduct of business at the organization.

- Separation of Duties—The segregation of responsibilities and duties with regard to the various functional components of the organization (in other words, Is there adequate separation of duties between or among related functions?).

- Information Control Policies—The handling of information within the organization or between the organization and outside entities. This concern is specifically related to the control of information flow and to who can have access to what information as well as how information should be disposed of or destroyed.

RESOURCES/ASSETS

The following resources/assets are those that should be reviewed during the general organizational control review. The definition for each of these assets, listed down the left vertical column of the matrix, is as follows:

- Administrative Control Policies—The plan of the organization and the procedures and records that are concerned with the decision processes leading to management's authorization of transactions. Further, this resource is directly associated with the responsibility for achieving the objectives of the organization and is the starting point for establishing control of transactions.

- Accounting Control Policies—The plan of the organization and the procedures and records that are concerned with the safeguarding of assets and the reliability of financial records. Consequently, the accounting control policies should be designed to provide reasonable assurances that transactions are executed in accordance with management's general or specific authorization, transactions are recorded to maintain accountability for assets, transactions are recorded to permit preparation of management reports and financial statements, access to assets is limited to authorized personnel only, and recorded accountability for assets can be compared with the existing assets.

- Overall Organization Structure—The overall structure of the organization. This resource encompasses the formal and the informal structures as well as the management controls and separation of duties that are involved with the organization's structure.

- Departmental Organization Structure—The structure of specific departments within the overall organization. The general controls for various departments and the structure of these departments should be reviewed. This resource specifically is intended to include any departments that are involved with data processing functions.

CONCERNS / EXPOSURES

RESOURCES / ASSETS

	MANAGEMENT CONTROL	MANAGEMENT REPORTING	FRAUD/ DEFALCATION	PRIVACY	SEPARATION OF DUTIES	INFORMATION CONTROL POLICIES				
ADMINISTRATIVE CONTROL POLICIES	14, 16, 17, 20-23, 26-30, 37, 44, 49	2, 12, 13, 36, 37, 49	2, 4, 5, 10, 13, 16, 18, 19, 24, 30, 34, 42, 45, 46, 47, 49	4, 5, 10, 13, 16, 18, 24, 30, 34, 38, 41, 42, 44, 45-47, 49	1, 5, 24, 34	2, 4, 34, 35, 38, 39-42, 44-47				
ACCOUNTING CONTROL POLICIES	7, 8, 14, 15, 20-23, 26-29, 37, 39, 49	2, 12, 13, 36, 37, 49	4, 5, 15, 42	4, 5, 41, 44	1, 16, 17	35, 39, 42, 44, 47				
OVERALL ORGANIZATION STRUCTURE	16, 20, 21, 35	20, 21, 35, 36	6, 16	6, 16	1, 6, 16	20, 21				
DEPARTMENTAL ORGANIZATION STRUCTURE	1, 3, 6, 11, 12, 17, 19. 20, 21, 23-29, 31-33	13, 20, 21, 23, 32	1, 3, 6, 17, 19, 25, 32, 33	1, 3, 6, 17, 19, 25, 33	1, 3, 5, 6, 10, 16, 17, 19, 24, 25, 30, 33	20, 21				
COMPUTER SECURITY ADMINISTRATION	7, 9, 15, 34, 37, 39, 43	2, 12, 36	2, 9, 10, 13, 34, 43, 45-48	13, 34, 42, 43, 45-48	10, 20, 45	9, 39, 43, 45-48				

FIGURE 2-1: GENERAL ORGANIZATIONAL CONTROL MATRIX

- Computer Security Administration—The overall administration and control of computer security, data processing departmental security, information control, data security, physical security, risk analysis, and any other security or privacy items that are related to data processing.

CONTROLS/SAFEGUARDS

The following controls/safeguards should be considered when reviewing the general organizational controls that should be in place within the organization. This numerical listing describes each control.

It should be noted that implementation of various controls can be both costly and time consuming. It is of great importance that a realistic and pragmatic evaluation be made with regard to the probability of a specific exposure affecting a specific asset. Only then can the control for safeguarding the asset be evaluated in a cost-effective manner.

The controls, as numerically listed in the cells of the matrix, are as follows:

1. Insure that there is adequate separation of duties between computer operators, application programmers, system programmers, and systems analysts. Whenever anyone but computer operations personnel enter the computer operations area and run the computer, insure that there are adequate outside controls so the proper management personnel are apprised of this special situation.

2. Consider saving a copy of the computer console log and the system output log for review at a later date. These two logs can serve as an audit trail as to what was inputted to the computer and the various operator commands.

3. Insure adequate separation of duties between manual data preparation and computer data reduction such as keypunching/keytaping/etc.

4. When running critical or sensitive jobs on the computer, use two or more computer operators and have someone from the user area present during the printout of the job.

5. When feasible, rotate computer operators between different job runs.

6. Organize the data processing function separately from other departments and especially have it separate from financial operations. Also, consider having the data processing operations (the people who run the daily computer jobs) totally separated from the systems and programming functions.

7. Insure that there is an overall disaster plan for data processing operations.

8. Insure that there is a formal approval system for program changes or system modifications (program change control policy).

9. Continually stress the "integrity of the individual" through education and training. This can best be done by continuous education of individuals in the areas of security and job efficiency.

10. As possible, insist that everyone take at least five consecutive days of vacation, so someone else can perform their job function (this is probably only necessary in sensitive or key positions).

11. Insure that there is an adequate job-run manual for each computer job. The

job-run manual should include at least job operating instructions, job setup information, notes on forms or other printer functions, and restart procedures/checkpoints in case of job failure.

12. Insure that there is some sort of a machine-utilization report to identify at least the job run, the computer operator present, whether or not the programmer was called, the elapsed computer time, and any unusual conditions encountered during the job run.

13. Insure that the departmental management reviews all control reports and resolves any exceptions as they occur.

14. Insure that there is adequate insurance coverage for loss of computer hardware, data processing media, and possibly for business interruption and extra expense, and that there are errors and omissions policies.

15. Conduct a risk analysis to identify critical programs (because of their higher likelihood of fraud) and closely control these programs or systems.

16. Provide for an operational control group that interfaces between the computer users and computer operations to control inputs, outputs, and resolve exceptions (data control).

17. Provide for a system test group that will adequately test all modifications to systems, as well as new systems that are being developed.

18. Develop a policy that will allow the termination of unsuitable employees immediately (provide severance pay rather than a two- or three-week notice).

19. Insure that there is adequate separation of duties within the user area being audited. This involves the separation of duties between individuals or between on-line terminal operators as they relate to the data processing application system being reviewed.

20. Review the organizational charts to insure that the organization is functional and can operate successfully within the confines of the overall organization.

21. Interrelate the overall organizational charts with the individual departmental organizational charts to insure that an adequate working relationship exists.

22. Review the general policies handed down by management with regard to the data processing operations.

23. Review the data processing department procedures to see if they are adequately following and/or carrying out the basic policies as depicted by the overall top management of the organization.

24. Review the job descriptions within the data processing department in order to insure that there is adequate separation of job functions; for example, computer operators should not be required to program.

25. Insure that there is adequate separation of duties between the personnel working in the tape/disk library and the other computer operations personnel.

26. Insure that the job-handling procedures within the data processing departent are written into a policy or standards manual.

27. Provide written scheduling procedures within the data processing operations.

28. Provide monthly processing schedules and cutoff dates within the data processing operation standards manual.

29. Provide written policies for batch-job submission and/or batch-job authorization.

30. When feasible, insure that the data processing operations personnel either review or add the job-control cards to batch jobs, so illegal jobs cannot be imbedded within a batch job.

31. Use both internal and external labels for tapes and disks when possible; it may be best to use a serial number only as the external label.

32. Insure that there is a computerized system for file release (tape and disk) so there is adequate control over this media so that the media does not get improperly erased.

33. Provide a separate tape/disk library area. This area should be separate from but contiguous to the data processing operations.

34. Provide adequate physical security and access control in order to insure that only authorized personnel get into the data processing department, and especially into the computer operations/tape library.

35. Insure that there is a special procedure for reporting troubles and for documenting problems. Systems should allow for the reporting of various problems to one central source, who will insure the prompt maintenance or repair of such.

36. Insist on system-utilization reports for various management personnel to review.

37. Provide a standard with regard to the system development life cycle (SDLC). This will insure a consistent methodology for developing systems and will allow the EDP auditor to review systems development at key project milestones.

38. Provide a separate standard with regard to data base administration. This standard should be utilized for data base development and continual control.

39. Insure that there is adequate documentation for all systems and programs.

40. Insure that any information concerning individuals or public relationships be disclosed to public sources only through specific designated personnel or specific departments.

41. Insure that any information that can be directly identified with an individual be released only upon that individual's written authority.

42. Insure that all sensitive computer-generated reports bear a heading that states that this report is private and confidential proprietary information, as well as bearing a statement as to how the report should be disposed of when it is no longer needed.

43. Designate an organizational spokesman as the Information Control Officer for the entire organization. This person is responsible for all data processing security, both data and physical.

44. Insure that the highest organizational office issues a general policy guideline for both security and privacy throughout the entire organization. This policy may take several forms and may be written in several sections in order to be more specific to the various organizational departments.

45. Insure that there is a specific written policy regarding who within the organization has the right of access to specific information. This policy should define any limitations on the use of this information by those approved for access.

46. Insure that there is a specific policy for the records of the organization, defining who will maintain the records, the environment in which they will be maintained, and providing a clear time limit and disposal plan for old records.

47. Clarify the policies as to who owns the data bases and the information contained therein as well as who has the authority to originate, modify, or delete existing data within the specific data bases.

48. Provide an organizationwide training program for security and privacy. This training program may take the form of specific training and also include a monthly or quarterly security and privacy newsletter.

49. Insure that there is an audit committee of outside directors that interacts with the audit function.

INPUT CONTROL MATRIX

This chapter defines and discusses the control review matrix to be used when reviewing the input controls of a data processing computerized record-keeping system. The controls/safeguards listed in this matrix are specifically designed for reviewing the transaction origination controls and transaction entry controls. Many of these controls may be oriented toward batch computer systems; therefore, the on-line terminal control matrix in chapter 7 should also be utilized.

THE MATRIX APPROACH

The internal control area to be reviewed using this matrix covers inputs to the computer system. These inputs may involve transaction origination or transaction entry and will be somewhat oriented toward batch computer systems (see chapter 7: On-Line Terminal Control Matrix, for the majority of the on-line input controls). When reviewing the input controls, match each resource/asset with its corresponding concern/exposure as listed in Figure 3-1: Input Control Matrix. This matrix lists the resources in relation to the potential exposures and cross-relates these with the various controls/safeguards that should be considered when reviewing inputs to computer systems (see chapter 1 for an explanation of how to use the control matrix approach).

Immediately following the matrix is a definition of each of the concerns/exposures that are listed across the top of the matrix and each of the resources/assets that are listed down the left vertical column of the matrix. Following these definitions is a complete numerical listing and description of each of the controls/safeguards that are listed numerically in the cells of the matrix.

CONCERNS/EXPOSURES

The following concerns/exposures are those that are directly applicable to the inputs (transaction origination and transaction entry) of a computer-based system. The definition for each of these exposures, listed across the top of the matrix, is as follows:

- Authorization—The proper authorization either prior to the input (source document) or during input into the computer system.

- Source Document Origination—The procedures and methods used to insure the proper and timely recording of data. The data may be recorded directly in a machine-readable form, or it may be recorded initially on a human-readable document.

- Source Document Error Handling—The procedures and methods used to insure that all manual transactions rejected at any point in the system are corrected and reentered in a timely manner.

- Source Document Retention—The procedures and methods used to insure the proper retention of source documents, including the adequate backup of source data maintained to provide audit trails or to be used for recovery should the computer data be inadvertently destroyed.

- Data Entry—The procedures and methods used to insure the proper collection of data for recording as well as the transcription of that data to a

CONCERNS / EXPOSURES

RESOURCES / ASSETS

	AUTHORIZATION	SOURCE DOCUMENT ORIGINATION	SOURCE DOCUMENT ERROR HANDLING	SOURCE DOCUMENT RETENTION	DATA ENTRY	TRANSACTION DATA VALIDATION	TRANSACTION ENTRY ERROR HANDLING	NEGOTIABLE DOCUMENT CONTROL	PRIVACY	
INPUT DEVICES		6, 10			10, 43, 41	10	39, 43		57	
OPERATIONAL PROCEDURES	5, 7, 9, 11-19, 25, 58	2,4,5,7,8,10, 13, 14, 20-25 31-34, 41, 44, 55, 57, 59-62	4,5,15,21,27,34 38,40-42,46,49, 50, 54, 56, 59, 64	15, 16, 29, 47, 48, 61, 63	1-8, 14, 20, 23, 24,27,28,30,31, 33,34,40,42,44, 45,54,55,57,59, 60, 62, 67, 68	1-3, 6, 8-10, 12, 25, 28, 31, 33, 35-38, 40 53, 56, 67, 68	21, 24, 28, 34 39, 40, 42, 49-56, 64	15-18, 26, 57	4, 9, 11, 15, 18, 20, 32, 46, 57, 58, 60, 61	
PEOPLE	5, 7, 9, 11-19, 25, 28	4,5,9,10,12-14, 20, 44, 45, 57, 59-62, 66	4,15,45, 46, 49, 50, 56, 59, 64, 65	15, 16, 29, 47, 48, 63	2,4,5,7,14,20, 23, 24, 27, 28, 40,44,45,54,55, 57, 59, 60, 62, 66	9, 10, 12, 25, 53, 56	24, 28, 49-56, 64, 65	15-18, 26, 57	4, 9, 11, 15, 18, 20, 32, 46, 57, 58, 60, 61	
FILES (MANUAL OR MAGNETIC MEDIA)		3, 4, 8, 9		15, 16, 29, 47, 48, 61, 63	3		51			
RECORDS STORAGE				15, 16, 29, 47, 48, 61, 63						
FORMS		22, 23, 30, 62	56	15, 16, 61	26, 62			15, 17, 18, 26		

FIGURE 3-1: INPUT CONTROL MATRIX

machine-readable form for input to the computer system. This begins after the source documents have been originated and authorized. At this point it is necessary to prepare the data further for data processing input.

- Transaction Data Validation—The validation of data as it enters the computerized system.

- Transaction Entry Error Handling—The methodologies and controls for handling errors after they have been entered into the system, correcting these errors, and reentering the corrected data into the system.

- Negotiable Document Control—The manual handling and use of negotiable document forms, either before, during, or after the use of these negotiable documents within the data processing department.

- Privacy—The accidental or intentional release of data about an individual, assuming that the release of this personal information was improper to the normal conduct of the business at the organization.

RESOURCES/ASSETS

The following resources/assets are those that should be reviewed during the input control review. The definition for each of these assets, listed down the left vertical column of the matrix, is as follows:

- Input Devices—Any or all of the input devices used to interconnect with the computer system. This would specifically include (without excluding other devices) key punches, keytape/disk units, card readers, tape and disk units, optical readers, local terminals, and the like.

- Operational Procedures—The written procedures to be followed during the origination of, preparation of, and inputting of data to the computerized system.

- People—The individuals responsible for preparing and inputting data, operating and maintaining the equipment, following the operational procedures, and performing any other operations during the input of data to the computerized system.

- Files (Manual or Magnetic Media)—The manual files of source documents and the data once it is stored upon magnetic devices such as magnetic tapes or disks.

- Records Storage—The long-term storage of various source documents or other types of data or programs that may be needed at some time in the future. This resource also includes the long-term storage of data that has been written onto microforms.

- Forms—Any of the specially designed and preprinted forms that might be utilized prior to or during the inputting of data to the computerized system.

CONTROLS/SAFEGUARDS

The following controls/safeguards should be considered when reviewing the inputs (transaction origination and transaction entry) of a computer-based system. This numerical listing describes each control.

It should be noted that implementation of various controls can be both costly and time consuming. It is of great importance that a realistic and pragmatic evaluation be made with regard to the probability of a specific exposure affecting a specific asset. Only then can the control for safeguarding the asset be evaluated in a cost-effective manner.

The controls, as numerically listed in the cells of the matrix, are as follows:

1. When keypunching or keytaping, use verification techniques to insure minimum errors. The operators might verify the entire data record or just critical fields.

2. Consider inputting critical fields twice when entering the data. In this way the computer system can match these two fields to insure correctness.

3. When using magnetic tape or magnetic disk as an input device, consider using both internal and external labels on the tape and disk media devices.

4. When source documents are passed between various departments for manual processing, log in these documents as to time received and from whom received as they move between these manual operations.

5. Perform a manual check of source documents for items such as control figures, prior editing, signature authorization, and the like.

6. Whenever self-checking numbers are used, consider building hardware into keypunch or keytape equipment to automatically verify these self-checking numbers during the input function.

7. Review the current operating procedures and verify that the handling procedures, signature authorization, and items similar to these are being followed during the manual handling of source documents or data input.

8. Log all inputs in sequence for on-line systems.

9. Use passwords for people and lockwords for files to protect from unauthorized data entry.

10. Restrict the access to various input devices.

11. Whenever feasible, segregate the functions of the generation of the transaction, the recording of the transaction, and the custody of the assets.

12. Consider establishing an independent control group to verify the authorization of transactions.

13. Insure that the function responsible for inputting the transaction verifies authorization signatures by comparing them to an authorized signature list.

14. Establish batch controls close to the point of input preparation to prevent introduction of unauthorized input between the source and the entry into the computerized system.

15. Store source documents in a locked cabinet to prevent unauthorized modifications or unauthorized use of the data prior to its entry into the system.

16. Restrict access to blank input forms and especially to negotiable documents.

17. Keep negotiable documents under lock and key and control them through the use of prior serial numbering.

18. Control sensitive documents and especially negotiable documents by using a dual custody method where two people must be present when the documents are being used. These two people should also perform a manual count, which would be reconciled by a third person back to the serial numbers that were preprinted on the negotiable documents.

19. Insure that the authorized individual does, in fact, sign source documents where this authorization is required.

20. Separate the computer operations functions from the transaction-generation and the transaction-recording functions.

21. Clearly describe the coding requirements, the batching requirements, and the scheduling requirements in the operations procedures manual.

22. Whenever possible, record data on a preprinted form to insure against errors and omissions.

23. When designing forms, insure that the data is recorded in a predetermined and uniform format in order to minimize errors and omissions.

24. Clearly describe the input keying requirements, response/error checking interpretation, and any special requirements in the operations procedures manual.

25. Insure that the personnel who input data either initial, sign, or identify the data that they prepare.

26. Design source documents with preprinted sequential serial numbers for control and to insure against lost documents.

27. Impose restrictions on batch size to allow ease of correction and control.

28. Record and/or maintain the identification number of the source document on the transaction to be processed.

29. Maintain the file of source documents by identification number or subject so it is readily retrievable. The identification number can be a preprinted sequential number or an assigned number such as employee number, part number, and the like.

30. Design and utilize precoded forms which contain information common to all given transaction types in order to reduce continual re-keying of the same data.

31. Include either the business date or processing date as a field in the input transaction.

32. Verify correctness of source documents prior to their conversion to a machine-readable form.

33. Include the Julian date as part of the transaction number.

34. Match transactions by processing cycle, and maintain uniqueness of batch and transaction numbers.

35. Assign transaction types to reflect the update process and desired update sequence.

36. Publish processing cycles to allow users to control cut-off dates.

37. Identify business or processing cut-off dates with specific logical accounting cycles.

38. Clearly define in the operations procedures the control points at which batch controls should be reconciled in the movement of data between and/or through various departments.

39. Establish backup processing procedures in case of a total and lengthy computer failure. These procedures should encompass alternative computers and/or manual data handling and processing procedures.

40. Insure that every department that handles data reconciles its batch controls, verifies the processing schedule to insure meeting cut-off points, and maintains a log of transactions passed between its department and other departments.

41. Try to centralize key-tape or key-disk operations close to the information source in order to insure against lost source documents.

42. Compare computer-produced batch totals, hash totals, transaction totals, sequence numbers, and the like to predetermined manually prepared totals.

43. Incorporate the batch-balancing comparison process into the key-tape or key-disk equipment.

44. Stamp the source document at the time of inputting to insure against inputting the same source documents twice.

45. Consider having a data control clerk visually verify all transactions prior to input, anticipate input, reasearch missing input, and the like.

46. Consider having a data control clerk maintain a log of all source documents returned to the user for correction. This log should be reviewed frequently to insure that the corrected document has been returned and reentered into the system.

47. Store source documents in a safe place. Filing of these documents should provide for rapid access to the documents.

48. Assign a retention date to each source document, and insure that it is placed in long-term storage which can be accessed at any time in the future.

49. Clearly outline the correction procedures in the operations manual. These procedures should include the types of errors that occur, correction procedures for all errors, and recycling of input and balancing of output reports.

50. Establish a central data control group responsible for error detection, correction, and resubmission.

51. Suspend the rejects on a file. Remove the file when the reentered corrected version is verified and accepted for processing.

52. In addition to the original error message, regularly print the overdue suspended items and their messages so follow-up can be done on errors that have not been corrected in a timely manner.

53. When reentering new transactions, edit the correction with the same module

used to edit the original transaction.

54. Provide adequate user manuals and operations procedure manuals that cover items such as how to prepare the documents, regulate document flow, adhere to cut-off schedules, describe input keying requirements, and the like.

55. Insure that each transaction to be entered into the computer system either has its own transaction identification or the batch identification from which it came.

56. Whenever possible, utilize a cross-reference field, in which the source document number might be part of the transaction identification. This will provide a cross-reference useful in tracing information to and from the source document.

57. Insure that there is adequate separation of duties during the data preparation and data inputting to the computer system.

58. Insure that there is evidence of approval (stamp the document) with regard to written authorizations and/or signatures.

59. Develop a control desk function to monitor the timely receipt of transactions and/or batches and to maintain proper source transaction schedules and compliance with requirements to the cut-offs.

60. Utilize a transmittal document to control the movement of paperwork between various users and the data entry function.

61. Physically secure input during the transportation of source documents and/or source data between work areas.

62. Utilize source turnaround documents to insure proper turnaround times. The turnaround portion of the document contains prerecorded data that can be used as the input medium for computer processing.

63. Develop a source document retention schedule and maintain a cross-index system so as to know how long to keep source documents and when to dispose of them. This can also be used for source document retrieval and for changing the retention dates, should it become necessary.

64. Develop written error-handling procedures to provide user personnel with comprehensive instructions for source document error detection, error correction, and corrected data resubmission.

65. Insure that the operations personnel receive adequate job training.

66. Periodically rotate the duties between the operations personnel to reduce boredom and to give new job duties to different personnel.

67. Insure that there are run-to-run totals so as not to lose data or information between jobs.

68. Cross-reference data input to record counts, control totals, hash totals, batch totals, and the like.

DATA COMMUNICATION CONTROL MATRIX

This chapter outlines the control review matrix to be used when reviewing the data communication network that interconnects remote terminals and the central computer system or the various portions of an on-line distributed network. The controls/safeguards listed in this matrix are specifically designed for review of the data communication network. This matrix should be used in conjunction with the control matrices in chapters 5 and 7.

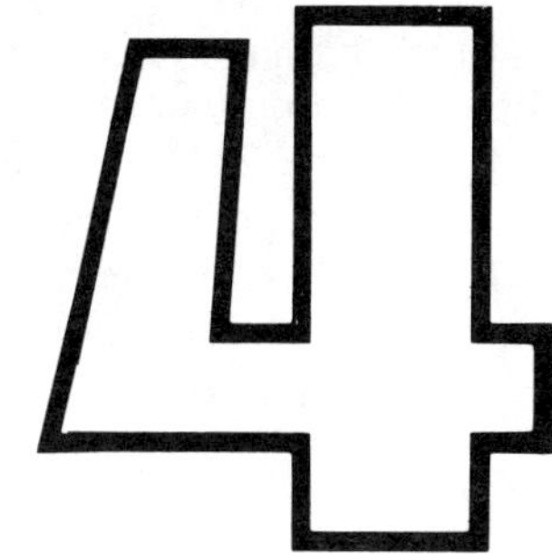

THE MATRIX APPROACH

The internal control area to be reviewed using this matrix covers the data communication links between the computer and the input/output terminals. These data-communication-oriented controls may involve hardware controls, software controls, and personnel controls. When reviewing the data communication controls, match each resource/asset with its corresponding concern/exposure as listed in Figure 4-1: Data Communication Control Matrix. This matrix lists the resources in relation to the potential exposures and cross-relates these with the various controls/safeguards that should be considered when reviewing the data communication controls (see chapter 1 for an explanation on how to use the control matrix approach).

Immediately following the matrix is a definition of each of the concerns/exposures that are listed across the top of the matrix and each of the resources/assets that are listed down the left vertical column of the matrix. Following these definitions is a complete numerical listing and description of each of the controls/safeguards that are listed numerically in the cells of the matrix.

CONCERNS/EXPOSURES

The following concerns/exposures are those that are directly applicable to the data communication network review of an on-line system. The definition for each of these exposures, listed across the top of the matrix, is as follows:

- Errors and Omissions—The accidental or intentional transmission of data that is in error, including the accidental or intentional omission of data that should have been entered or transmitted on the on-line system. This type of exposure includes, but is not limited to, inaccurate data, incomplete data, malfunctioning hardware, and the like.

- Message Loss or Change—The loss of messages as they are transmitted throughout the data communication system, or the accidental/intentional changing of messages during transmission.

- Disasters and Disruptions (natural and man-made)—The temporary or long-term disruption of normal data communication capabilities. This exposure renders the organization's normal data communication on-line system inoperative.

- Privacy—The accidental or intentional release of data about an individual, assuming that the release of this personal information was improper to the normal conduct of the business at the organization.

- Security/Theft—The security or theft of information that should have been kept confidential because of its proprietary nature. In a way, this is a form of privacy, but the information removed from the organization does not pertain to an individual. The information might be inadvertently (accidentally) released, or it might be the subject of an outright theft. This exposure also includes the theft of assets such as might be experienced in embezzlement, fraud, or defalcation.

- Reliability (Up-Time)—The reliability of the data communication network and its "up-time." This includes the organization's ability to keep the data communication network operating and the mean time between failures (MTBF) as well as the time to repair equipment when it malfunctions. Reliability of hardware, reliability of software, and the maintenance of these two items are chief concerns here.

- Recovery and Restart—The recovery and restart capabilities of the data communication network, should it fail. In other words, How does the software operate in a failure mode? How long does it take to recover from a failure? This recovery and restart concern also includes backup for key portions of the data communication network and the contingency planning for backup, should there be a failure at any point of the data communication network.

- Error Handling—The methodologies and controls for handling errors at a remote distributed site or at the centralized computer site. This may also involve the error handling procedures of a distributed data processing system (at the distributed site). The object here is to insure that when errors are discovered they are promptly corrected and reentered into the system for processing.

- Data Validation and Checking—The validation of data either at the time of transmission or during transmission. The validation may take place at a remote site (intelligent terminal), at the central site (front-end communication processor), or at a distributed intelligence site (concentrator or remote front-end communication processor).

RESOURCES/ASSETS

The following resources/assets are those that should be reviewed during the data communication control review. The definition for each of these assets, listed down the left vertical column of the matrix, is as follows:

- Central System—Most prevalent in the form of a central computer to which the data communication network transmits and from which it receives information. In a distributed system, with equal processing at each distributed node, there might not be an identifiable central system (just some other equal-sized distributed computer).

- Software—The software programs that operate the data communication network. These programs may reside in the central computer, a distributed-system computer, the front-end communication processor, a remote concentrator or statistical multiplexer, and/or a remote intelligent terminal. This software may include the telecommunications access methods, an overall teleprocessing monitor, programs that reside in the front-end processors, and/or programs that reside in the intelligent terminals.

CONCERNS / EXPOSURES

RESOURCES / ASSETS

	ERRORS AND OMISSIONS	MESSAGE LOSS OR CHANGE	DISASTERS AND DISRUPTIONS	PRIVACY	SECURITY/ THEFT	RELIABILITY (UP-TIME)	RECOVERY AND RESTART	ERROR HANDLING	DATA VALIDATION AND CHECKING	
CENTRAL SYSTEM	1-4, 7, 39,41-43, 47, 48	1-5, 7, 37, 39, 48, 49, 89	1, 8, 11, 13, 16, 29, 40, 48, 50, 51, 54, 57, 58, 64, 65, 79, 85	6, 8, 24, 35, 53, 56, 60, 62, 68, 70, 72-74, 78-80	6, 8, 24, 35, 53, 56,60,62,68,70, 72-74, 77-80	1, 13,16,29,38, 40, 50, 51, 63-65, 68 81, 88	50, 51, 63-65, 68	48, 85, 89	6, 24, 39, 41, 47, 88	
SOFTWARE	1-4, 7,39,41-43, 46-49, 52	1-5, 7, 37, 39, 41, 42, 48, 49, 52, 54, 89	1, 8, 16, 40, 48, 50-54, 57-59, 63, 85	6, 8, 24, 35, 53, 56, 60, 62, 68, 70, 72-74, 78-80	6, 8, 24, 35, 39, 53, 56, 60, 62 68, 70, 72-74 78-80	1, 38, 40, 50, 51, 56-59, 61, 63, 68, 88	50-52, 61, 63, 64, 68	48, 61, 85, 89	6, 24, 39, 41, 47-49, 52, 53, 55, 60, 88	
FRONT-END COMMUNICATION PROCESSOR	1-4, 7, 34, 39, 41-44, 46-48	1-5, 7, 34, 37, 39, 41, 42, 49, 89	1,8,13,16,29, 40,44,48,50,51, 54, 57, 58, 64, 65, 79, 85	6, 8, 24, 35, 37, 45, 60, 62, 68, 70, 72-74 78-80	6, 8, 24, 29, 35, 37, 39, 45, 60, 62, 68, 70, 72-74, 78-80	1, 13, 16, 29, 30, 34, 36, 40, 43, 44, 50, 51, 63-65, 81, 88	37, 50, 51, 63-65	43, 48, 85, 89	6, 24, 39, 41, 45, 47, 48, 88	
MULTIPLEXER, CONCENTRATOR SWITCH	1-4, 7, 37, 39, 41, 44, 46, 47	1-5, 7, 37, 39, 41, 42, 49, 89	1, 8, 13, 16, 29, 30, 32, 33, 40, 44, 48, 50, 51, 54, 57, 58, 65, 79, 85	6, 8, 24, 35, 37, 45, 60, 62, 68, 70, 72-74 78-80	6, 8, 24, 29, 35, 37, 39, 45, 60, 62, 68, 70, 72-74, 78-80	1, 13, 16, 29,30, 32-34, 36, 40, 44, 50, 51, 63-65, 81, 88	37, 50, 51, 63, 64	48, 85, 89	6, 24, 39, 41, 45, 47, 48, 88	
COMMUNICATION CIRCUITS (LINES)	12, 26	28, 70, 91	10, 15, 16, 18, 26, 63, 64, 66, 75, 76, 79, 91	25, 28, 68, 70 75, 76, 78-80 91	25, 28, 68, 70 75, 76, 78-80, 91	15, 16, 20, 21, 23, 26, 27, 63, 64, 66-68, 88	63, 64, 66, 68	85		
LOCAL LOOP	12	25	25, 75, 85	25, 76	25, 29, 75, 76	68, 88	63, 64, 68	85		
MODEMS	12, 18	18, 24	8-11, 13-16, 18	24	24, 29	9-11, 13-18, 20, 21, 23, 36, 88	9-11, 14, 15, 63, 64	18-20, 22, 23		
PEOPLE	5, 39	5, 7, 31, 39, 70	79-87	6, 8, 24, 53, 69-71, 74, 77, 79, 80	6, 8, 24, 29, 53, 69-71, 74, 77, 79, 80	81, 82, 85-87	50, 51, 86, 87,	49, 86, 87, 89, 90	6, 88	
TERMINALS/ DISTRIBUTED INTELLIGENCE		2		6, 8, 24, 45, 53, 56, 62, 70	6, 8, 24, 29, 45, 53, 56, 62, 70	1, 40, 88	63, 64		6, 24, 45	

SEE CHAPTER 7 FOR MOST OF THESE CONTROLS

FIGURE 4-1: DATA COMMUNICATION CONTROL MATRIX

- Front-End Communication Processor—A hardware device that interconnects all the data communication circuits (lines) to the central computer or distributed computers and performs a subset of the following functions: code and speed conversion, protocol, error detection and correction, format checking, authentication, data validation, statistical data gathering, polling/addressing, insertion/deletion of line control codes, and the like.

- Multiplexer, Concentrator, Switch—Hardware devices that enable the data communication network to operate in the most efficient manner. The multiplexer is a device that combines, in one data stream, several simultaneous data signals from independent stations. The concentrator performs the same functions as a multiplexer except it is intelligent and therefore can perform some of the functions of a front-end communication processor. A *switch* is a device that allows the interconnection between any two circuits (lines) connected to the switch. There might be two distinct types of switch: a switch that performs message switching between stations (terminals) might be located within the data communication network facilities that are owned and operated by the organization; a circuit or line switching switch that interconnects various circuits might be located at (and owned by) the telephone company central office. For example, organizations perform message switching and the telephone company performs circuit switching.

- Communication Circuits (Lines)—The common carrier facilities used as links (a link is the interconnection of any two stations/terminals) to interconnect the organization's stations/terminals. These communication circuits include, not to the exclusion of others, satellite facilities, public switched dial-up facilities, point-to-point private lines, multiplexed lines, multipoint or loop configured private lines, WATS services, and many others.

- Local Loop—The communication facility between the customer's premises and the telephone company's central office or the central office of any other special common carrier. The local loop is usually assumed to be metallic pairs of wires.

- Modems—A hardware device used for the conversion of data signals from terminals (digital signal) to an electrical form (analog signal) which is acceptable for transmission over the communication circuits that are owned and maintained by the telephone company or other special common carrier.

- People—The individuals responsible for inputting data, operating and maintaining the data communication network equipment, writing the software programs for the data communications, managing the overall data communication network, and those involved at the remote stations/terminals.

- Terminals/Distributed Intelligence—Any or all of the input or output devices used to interconnect with the on-line data communication network. This resource would specifically include, without excluding other devices, teleprinter terminals, video terminals, remote job entry terminals, transaction terminals, intelligent terminals, and any other devices used with distributed data communication networks. These may include microprocessors or minicomputers when they are input/output devices or if they are used to control portions of the data communication network.

CONTROLS/SAFEGUARDS

The following controls/safeguards should be considered when reviewing the data communication network review of an on-line system. This numerical listing describes each control.

It should be noted that implementation of various controls can be both costly and time consuming. It is of great importance that a realistic and pragmatic evaluation be made with regard to the probability of a specific exposure affecting a specific asset. Only then can the control for safeguarding the asset be evaluated in a cost-effective manner.

The controls, as numerically listed in the cells of the matrix, are as follows:

1. Insure that the system can switch messages destined for a down station/terminal to an alternate station/terminal.

2. Determine whether the system can perform message-switching to transmit messages between stations/terminals.

3. In order to avoid lost messages in a message-switching system, provide a store and forward capability. This is where a message destined for a busy station is stored at the central switch and then forwarded at a later time when the station is no longer busy.

4. Review the message or transaction logging capabilities to reduce lost messages, provide for an audit trail, restrict messages, prohibit illegal messages, and the like. These messages might be logged at the remote station (intelligent terminal), they might be logged at a remote concentrator/remote front-end processor, or they might be logged at the central front-end communication processor/central computer.

5. Transmit messages promptly to reduce risk of loss.

6. Identify each message by the individual user's password, the terminal, and the individual message sequence number.

7. Acknowledge the successful or unsuccessful receipt of all messages.

8. Utilize physical security controls throughout the data communication network (see chapter 8: Physical Security Control Matrix). This includes the use of locks, guards, badges, sensors, alarms, and administrative measures to protect the physical facilities, data communication networks, and related data communication equipment. These safeguards are required for access monitoring and control to protect data communication equipment and software from damage by accident, fire, and environmental hazard either intentional or unintentional.

9. Consider using modems that have either manual or remote actuated loopback switches for fault isolation to insure the prompt identification of malfunctioning equipment. These are extremely important in order to increase the up-time and to identify faults.

10. Use front panel lights on modems to indicate if the circuit/line is functioning properly (carrier signal is up). This may not be a viable alternative with organizations that have hundreds of modems.

11. Consider a modem with alternate voice capabilities for quick trouble-shooting between the central site and a major remote site.

12. When feasible, use digital data transmission, because it has a lower error rate than analog data transmission.

13. For data communication equipment, check the manufacturer's mean time

between failures (MTBF) in order to insure that the data communication equipment has the largest MTBF.

14. Consider placing unused backup modems in critical areas of the data communication network.

15. Consider using modems that have an automatic or semiautomatic dial backup capability in case the leased line fails.

16. Review the maintenance contract and mean time to fix (MTTF) for all data communication equipment. Maintenance should be both fast and available. Determine from where the maintenance is dispatched, and determine if tests can be made from a remote site (for example, in many cases modems have remote loopback capabilities).

17. Increase data transmission efficiency. The faster the modem synchronization time, the lower will be the turnaround time and thus more throughput to the system.

18. Consider modems with automatic equalization (built in microprocessors for circuit equalization and balancing) in order to compensate for amplitude and phase distortions on the line. This will reduce the number of errors in transmission and may decrease the need for conditioned lines.

19. With regard to the efficiency of modems, review to see if they have multiple-speed switches so the transmission rate can be lowered when the line error rates are high.

20. Utilize four-wire circuits in a pseudo-full duplex transmission mode. In other words, keep the carrier wave up in each direction on alternate pairs of wires in order to reduce turnaround time and gain efficiency during transmission.

21. If needed, use full duplex transmission on two-wire circuits with special modems that split the frequencies and thus achieve full duplex transmission.

22. Increase the speed of transmission. The faster the speed of transmission by the modem, the more cost effective are the data communications, but error rates may increase with speed, and therefore you may need more error detection and correction facilities.

23. Utilize a reverse channel capability for control signals (supervisory) and to keep the carrier wave up in both directions.

24. Consider the following special controls on dial-up modems when the data communication network allows incoming dial-up connections: change the phone numbers at regular intervals; keep the phone numbers confidential; remove the phone numbers from the modems in the computer operations area; require that each "dial-up terminal" have an electronic identification circuit chip to transmit its unique identification to the front-end communication processor; do not allow automatic call receipt and connection (always have a person intercept the call and make a verbal identification); have the central site call the various terminals that will be allowed connection to the system; utilize dial-out only where an incoming dialed call triggers an automatic dial-back to the caller (in this way the central system controls those phone numbers to which it will allow connection).

25. Physically trace out and, as best as possible, secure the local loop communi-

cation circuits/lines within the organization or facility. After these lines leave the facility and enter the public domain, they cannot be physically secured.

26. Consider conditioning the voice-grade circuits in order to reduce the number of errors during transmission (this may be unnecessary with the newer microprocessor-based modems that perform automatic equalization and balancing).

27. Use four-wire circuits in such a fashion that there is little to no turnaround time. This can be done by using two wires in each direction and keeping the carrier signal up.

28. Within an organizational facility, fiber optics (laser) communication circuits can be used so as to totally preclude the possibility of wiretapping.

29. Insure that there is adequate physical security at remote sites and especially for terminals, concentrators, multiplexers, and front-end communication processors.

30. Determine whether the multiplexer/concentrator/remote front-end hardware has redundant logic and backup power supplies with automatic fall-back capabilities in case the hardware fails. This will increase the up-time of the many stations/terminals that might be connected to this equipment.

31. Consider logging inbound and outbound messages at the remote site.

32. Consider uninterruptible power supplies at large multiplexer/concentrator type remote sites.

33. Consider multiplexer/concentrator equipment that has diagnostic lights, diagnostic capabilities, and the like.

34. If a concentrator is being used, is it performing some of the controls that are usually performed by the front-end communication processor and therefore increasing the efficiency and correctness of data transmissions?

35. See if the polling configuration list can be changed during the day in order to exclude or include specific terminals. This would allow the positive exclusion of a terminal as well as allowing various terminals to come on-line and off-line during the working day.

36. Can the front-ends, concentrators, modems, and the like handle the automatic answering and automatic outward dialing of calls? This would increase the efficiency and accuracy when it is preprogammed into the system.

37. Insure that all inbound and outbound messages are logged by the central processor, the front-end, or remote concentrator in order to insure against lost messages, keep track of message sequence numbers (identify illegal messages), and to use for system restart should the entire system crash.

38. For efficiency, insure that the central system can address either a group of terminals (group address), several terminals at a time (multiple address), one terminal at a time (single address), or send a broadcast message simultaneously to all stations/terminals in the system.

39. See that each inbound and outbound message is serial numbered as well as time and date stamped at the time of logging.

40. Insure that there is a "time out" facility so the system does not get hung up trying to poll/address a station. Also, if a particular station "times out" four or five consecutive times, it should be removed from the network configuration polling list so time is not wasted on this station (improves communication efficiency).

41. Consider having concentrators and front-ends perform two levels of editing. In the first level the front-end may add items to a message, reroute the message, or rearrange the data for further transmission. It may also check a message address for accuracy and perform parity checks. In the second level of editing, the concentrator or front-end is programmed to perform specific edits of the different transactions that enter the system. This editing is an application system type of editing and deals with message content rather than form and is specific to each application program being executed.

42. Have the concentrators, front-ends, and central computers handle the message priority system, if one exists. A priority system is set up to permit a higher line utilization to certain areas of the network or to insure that certain transactions are handled before other transactions of lesser importance.

43. See that the front-end collects message traffic statistics and performs correlations of traffic density and circuit availability. These analyses are mandatory for the effective management of a large data communication network. Some of the items included in a traffic density report might be the number of messages handled per hour or per day on each link of the network, the number of errors encountered per hour or per day, the number of errors encountered per program or per program module, the terminals or stations that appear to have a higher than average error record, and the like.

44. Insure that the front-ends and concentrators can perform miscellaneous functions such as triggering remote alarms if certain parameters are exceeded, performing multiplexing operations internally, signaling abnormal occurrences to the central computer, slowing up input/output messages when the central computer is overburdened due to heavy traffic, and the like.

45. Insure that the concentrators and front-ends can validate electronic terminal identification.

46. Insure that there is a message intercept function for inoperable terminals or invalid terminal addresses.

47. See that messages are checked for valid destination address.

48. Insure adequate error detection and control capabilities. These might include echo-checking, where a message is transmitted to a remote site and the remote site echoes the message back for verification, or it might include forward error correction, where special hardware boxes can automatically correct some errors upon receipt of the message, or it might include detection with retransmission. Detection with retransmission is the most common and cost-effective form of error detection and correction. This may include identification of errors by reviewing the parity bit or utilizing a special code to identify errors in individual characters during transmission. A more prevalent form is to utilize a polynomial (mathematical algorithm) to detect errors in message blocks. Whichever way is used, when a message error is detected, it is retransmitted until it is received correctly.

49. When reviewing error detection in transmission, first determine whatever error rate can be tolerated, then determine the extent and pattern of errors on the communication links used by the organization, and then review the error detection and correction methodologies in use and determine if they are adequate for the application systems utilizing the data communication network. In other words, a purely administrative message network (no critical financial data) would not require error detection and correction capabilities equal to a network that transmits critical financial data.

50. Insure that there are adequate restart and recovery software routines to recover from items such as a trapped machine check, where instead of bringing down the entire data communication system, a quick recovery can be made and only the one transaction need be retransmitted.

51. Insure that there are adequate restart and recovery procedures to effect both a warm start and a cold start. In other words, a data communication system should never completely fail so the user has to perform a cold start (start up as if it is a new day, all message counters cleared). The system should go into a warm start procedure, where only parts of the system are disabled and recovery can be made while the system is operating in a degraded mode.

52. Insure that there is an audit trail logging facility to assist in the reconstruction of data files and the reconstruction of transactions from the various stations. There should be the capability to trace back to the terminal and user.

53. Provide some tables for checking for access by terminals, people, data base, and programs. These tables should be in protected areas of memory.

54. Safe store all messages. All transactions/messages should be protected in case of a disastrous situation, such as power failure.

55. Protect against concurrent file updates. If the data management software does not provide this protection, the data communication software should.

56. For convenience, flexibility, and security, insure that terminals can be brought up or down dynamically while the system is running.

57. Make available a systems trace capability to assist in locating problems.

58. Insure that the documentation of the system software is comprehensive.

59. Provide adequate maintenance for the software programs.

60. Insure that the system supports password protection (multilevel password protection).

61. Identify all default options in the software and their impact if they do not operate properly.

62. For entering sensitive or critical systems commands, restrict these commands to one master input terminal and insure strict physical custody over this terminal. In other words, restrict those personnel who can use this terminal.

63. Insure that there are adequate recovery facilities and/or capabilities for a software failure, loss of key pieces of hardware, and loss of various communication circuit/lines.

64. Insure that there are adequate backup facilities (local and remote) to back up key pieces of hardware and communication circuits/lines.

65. Consider backup power capabilities for large facilities such as the central site and various remote concentrators.

66. Consider installing the capabilities to fall back to the public dial network from a leased line configuration.

67. When utilizing multidrop or loop circuits, review the up-time problems. These types of configurations are more cost-effective than point-to-point configurations, but when there is a circuit failure close to the central site, all terminals/stations downline are disconnected.

68. Review the physical security (local and remote) for circuits/lines (especially the local loop), hardware/software, physical facilities, storage media, and the like.

69. For personnel that work in critical or sensitive areas, consider enforcing the following policies: insist that they take at least five consecutive days of vacation per year, check with their previous employers, perform an annual credit check, and have them sign hiring agreements stating that they will not sell programs, etc.

70. With regard to data security, consider encrypting all messages transmitted.

71. Develop an overall organizational security policy for the data communication network. This policy should specifically cover the security and privacy of information.

72. Insure that all sensitive communication programs and data are stored in protected areas of memory or disk storage.

73. Insure that all communication programs or data, when they are off-line, are stored in areas with adequate physical security.

74. Insure that all communication programs and data are adequately controlled when they are transferred to microfiche.

75. Lock up phone equipment rooms and install alarms on the doors of those phone equipment rooms that contain the basic data communication circuits.

76. Do not put communication lines through the public switchboard unless it is a new electronic switchboard (ESS) and the intent is to gain verbal identification of incoming dial-up data communication calls.

77. Review the communication system's console log that shows "network supervisor terminal commands" such as: disable or enable a line or station for input or output, alternately route traffic from one station to another, change the order and/or frequency of line or terminal service (polling, calling, dialing), and the like.

78. Consider packet-switching networks which use alternate routes for different packets of information from the same message; this would offer a form of security in case someone were intercepting messages.

79. Insure that there is a policy for the use of test equipment. Modern-day test equipment may offer a new vulnerability to the organization. This test equipment is easily connected to communication lines, and all messages can be read in clear "English language." Test equipment should not be used for monitoring lines "for fun"; it should be locked up (key lock or locked hood) when it is not in use and after normal working hours when it is not needed for testing and debugging; programs written for programmable test equipment should be kept locked up and out of the hands of those who do not need these programs.

80. Review the operational procedures, for example, the administrative regulations, policies, and day-to-day activities supporting the security/safeguards of the data communication network. These procedures may include:

- Specifying the objectives of the EDP security for an organization, espeially as they relate to data communications.

- Planning for contingencies of security "events," including recording of all exception conditions and activities.

- Assuring management that other safeguards are implemented, maintained, and audited, including background checks, security clearances and hiring of people with adequate security oriented characteristics; separation of duties; mandatory vacations.

- Developing effective safeguards for deterring, detecting, preventing, and correcting undesirable security events.

- Reviewing the cost-effectiveness of the system and the related benefits such as better efficiency, improved reliability, and economy.

- Looking for the existence of current administrative regulations, security plans, contingency plans, risk analysis, personnel understanding of management objectives, and then reviewing the adequacy and timeliness of the specified procedures in satisfying these.

81. Review the preventive maintenance and scheduled diagnostic testing such as cleaning, replacement, and inspection of equipment to evaluate its accuracy, reliability, and integrity. This may include schedules for testing and repair, adequate testing of software program changes submitted by the vendor, inventories of replacement parts (circuit boards), past maintenance records, and the like.

82. Determine whether there is a central site for reporting all problems encountered in the data communication network. This usually results in faster repair time.

83. Review the financial protection afforded from insurance for various hardware, software, and data stored on magnetic media.

84. Review the legal contracts with regard to the agreements for performing a specific service and a specific costing basis for the data communication network hardware and software. These might include bonding of employees, conflict of interest agreements, clearances, nondisclosure agreements, agreements establishing liability for specific security events by vendors, agreements by vendors not to perform certain acts that would incur a penalty, and the like.

85. Review the organization's fault isolation/diagnostics, including the techniques used to ascertain the integrity of the various hardware/software components comprising the total data communication entity. These techniques are used to audit, review, and control the total data communication environment and to isolate the offending elements either on a periodic basis or upon detection of a failure. These techniques may include diagnostic software routines, electrical loopback, test message generation, administrative and personnel procedures, and the like.

86. Review the training and education of employees with regard to the data communication network. Employees must be adequately trained in this area because of the high technical competence required for data communication networks.

87. Insure that there is adequate documentation, including a precise description of programs, hardware, system configurations, and procedures intended to assist in the prevention of problems, identification of problems, and recovery from problems. The documentation should be sufficiently detailed to assist in reconstructing the system from its parts.

88. Review the techniques for testing used to validate the hardware and software operation to insure integrity. Testing, including that of personnel, should uncover departures from the specified operation.

89. Review error recording to reduce lost messages. All errors in transmission of messages in the system should be logged and this log should include the type of error, the time and date, the terminal, the circuit, the terminal operator, and the number of times the message was retransmitted before it was correctly received.

90. Review the error correction procedures. A user's manual should specify a cross-reference of error messages to the appropriate error code generated by the system. These messages help the user interpret the error that has occurred and suggest the corrective action to be taken. Insure that the errors are in fact corrected and the correct data reentered into the system.

91. Consider backing up key circuits/lines. This circuit backup may take the form of a second leased line, modems that have the ability to go to the public dial-up network when a leased line fails, or manual procedures where the remote stations can transmit verbal messages using the public dial-up network.

PROGRAM/COMPUTER PROCESSING CONTROL MATRIX

This chapter outlines the control review matrix that might be used when reviewing the programmed computer processing controls. The controls/safeguards listed in this matrix are specifically designed for reviewing the internal computer processing, the application programs (system software matrix is discussed in chapter 10), as well as the manual controls that are interrelated to computer processing and the associated applications programs. The various controls listed in this matrix will be applicable in some cases to batch systems and in other cases to on-line systems.

THE MATRIX APPROACH

The internal control area to be reviewed using this matrix covers program/computer processing controls. These program/computer processing controls involve those automated controls that can be built into computer programs and into computerized systems. When reviewing the program/computer processing controls, match each resource/asset with its corresponding concern/exposure as listed in Figure 5-1: Program/Computer Processing Control Matrix. This matrix lists the resources in relation to the potential exposures and cross-relates these with the various controls/safeguards that should be considered when reviewing the programmed controls in a system (see chapter 1 for an explanation of how to use the control matrix approach).

Immediately following the matrix is a definition of each of the concerns/exposures that are listed across the top of the matrix and each of the resources/assets that are listed down the left vertical column of the matrix. Following these definitions is a complete numerical listing and description of each of the controls/safeguards that are listed numerically in the cells of the matrix.

CONCERNS/EXPOSURES

The following concerns/exposures are those that are directly applicable to the program/computer processing of either on-line or batch systems. The definition for each of these exposures, listed across the top of the matrix, is as follows:

- Program Errors and Omissions—The accidental or intentional creation of an error during the processing of the data or the running of the application programs, including the accidental or intentional omission of data (loss) during the processing of a computer program. This type of exposure includes, but is not limited to, multiprogram code, trapped machine checks where programs just quit processing, loss of data during the running of a program, and the like.

- Unauthorized Program Changes—The temporary or permanent change of program code by individuals who are unauthorized to make these changes, as well as by individuals who are so authorized but who make illegal program changes for whatever reason.

- Security/Theft—The security or theft of information or programs that should have been kept confidential because of their proprietary nature. In a way, this is a form of privacy, but the information removed from the organization does not specifically pertain to an individual. The information or computer programs might be inadvertently (accidentally) removed from the organization or might be the subject of outright theft.

- Data Validation—The computer program editing of data prior to its processing and the preprogrammed specific actions that should be taken when erroneous data is discovered (this may also include the discovery of omissions in certain data that should have been included).

- Hardware Errors—The malfunctioning of the computer hardware so it appears that a program has made some sort of an error in processing. The concern here is that a hardware malfunction may cause erroneous data, data omissions, loss of specific data, and the like.

- Restart and Recovery—The restarting of computer programs that have failed during their normal course of processing and the recovery that should take place so no data is lost, erroneously processed, or processed twice because of the failure (the failure may have been caused by program failure or computer hardware failures).

- Audit Trails—Insurance that the processing of the data can be traced backward and forward through the entire computer processing cycle.

- Computer Program Generated Transactions—Insurance that any transactions that are automatically generated within an on-line system are adequately controlled. In other words, some on-line systems automatically create transactions during the time they are being run and these transactions should have adequate controls to prevent errors, erroneous transactions, and illegal transactions.

- Error Handling—The procedures and methods used to insure that all transactions or data that are rejected during the computer processing are, in fact, corrected and reentered into the system in a timely manner. This involves accounting for and detecting data errors, loss, or the nonprocessing of transactions, as well as the reporting of these errors, error correction, and the corrected data resubmission.

RESOURCES/ASSETS

The following resources/assets are those that should be reviewed during the program/computer processing control review. The definition for each of these assets, listed down the left vertical column of the matrix, is as follows:

- Application Programs and Systems—Any or all the computer programs that are utilized in the data processing operations. This resource should also be viewed as the overall macrosystems that operate within the organization (these systems may be made up of a group of computer programs). This is far and away the most valuable asset of the organization because, in the long run, the computer programs are more costly than the hardware upon which they operate.

CONCERNS / EXPOSURES

RESOURCES / ASSETS

	PROGRAM ERRORS AND OMISSIONS	UNAUTHORIZED PROGRAM CHANGES	SECURITY/ THEFT	DATA VALIDATION	HARDWARE ERRORS	RESTART AND RECOVERY	AUDIT TRAILS	COMPUTER PROGRAM GENERATED TRANS—ACTIONS	ERROR HANDLING	
APPLICATION PROGRAMS AND SYSTEMS	1-9, 16–20, 63, 71-74, 86, 89, 90	13, 22, 23, 25, 30-33, 35, 38, 43, 44, 49-51, 70, 85, 88, 90, 92	24, 25, 30-35, 38, 43, 49, 62, 70	2-8, 16, 69, 72-74, 89	70, 72-74, 89	20, 76, 77	6, 16, 22, 23, 25-28, 30, 32, 33, 35, 43,49	1,5,7,43,44, 51, 64, 65, 67, 68, 70, 71, 90,	9-15, 45, 71 78-81, 83	
DATA RECORD INTEGRITY	1,3-7,16,17, 27,69,71,73, 74, 80, 81	30-33	24-26, 29, 30-35, 38, 39, 48, 49	1-5, 7, 10, 12-14, 16, 17, 24, 25, 27, 28, 63, 69	41, 46, 47, 72, 87	20, 21, 28	6, 16, 25-28, 31, 32, 49, 64 66, 80-82	64-68	10-15, 45, 79-83	
OUTPUT INTEGRITY	2-4, 6, 7, 16, 18-20, 27, 69, 71, 73, 74, 80, 81	39	24-26, 29-35, 38, 39, 48, 49	2, 4-7, 9, 10, 16, 28, 69		2l, 28	17	64, 65, 67, 81	15, 71, 75, 78-83	
CENTRAL SYSTEM	16, 40-42, 46, 47, 69, 76, 77, 91	36-39, 48, 49, 51-53, 85, 86, 91	36-39, 42, 47-49, 51-53, 55, 62, 84, 91	16, 40, 69	46, 54-61, 87	42, 76, 77	30, 33, 42, 84, 91		91	
SOFTWARE PROGRAMS	1, 86, 87, 90	13, 22, 23, 25 30-33, 35, 38 44,49,50,51,70 85, 88-90, 92	24, 25, 30-35, 38, 49, 62, 70	89	70, 87, 89			51, 70, 90		

SEE CHAPTER 10 FOR MOST OF THESE CONTROLS

FIGURE 5-1: PROGRAM/COMPUTER PROCESSING CONTROL MATRIX

- Data Record Integrity—The data that is stored in the computer files or data bases and is used in the everyday processing of the organization's computerized record-keeping system.

- Output Integrity—The believability and integrity of the output reports from the system. The auditor should review this resource to insure that the output reports are Consistent, Accurate, Timely, Economic, and Relevant to the intended purpose (reports that meet these criteria will CATER to the needs of the organization).

- Central System—Most prevalent in the form of a central computer in which the computer programs operate. This asset may be in the form of a central computer system, or it may be in the form of numerous computer systems spread around in a distributed network.

- Software Programs—The software programs that run the overall computerized systems. These may include the operating system software (usually supplied by the computer vendor) as well as the software programs utilized to maintain and operate the data communication network, or the data base system (data management software). These software programs usually operate at the "systems control level" because any controls that are built into, or programmed into, this level of software affect all application programs. For example, a control that is built into the operating system software, data communication control software, or data management software would have its effect upon any incoming transaction that passed through that level of software programs without regard to whether it was a payroll transaction, inventory control transaction, financial balancing transaction, or the like.

CONTROLS/SAFEGUARDS

The following controls/safeguards should be considered when reviewing the programs or computer processing of either on-line or batch systems. This numerical listing describes each control.

It should be noted that implementation of various controls can be both costly and time consuming. It is of great importance that a realistic and pragmatic evaluation be made with regard to the probability of a specific exposure affecting a specific asset. Only then can the control for safeguarding the asset be evaluated in a cost-effective manner.

The controls, as numerically listed in the cells of the matrix, are as follows:

1. Transactions that are consecutively numbered by the station transmitting (these might be computer generated transactions) to the computer should be sequence number checked by the computer programs. In other words, the computer programs should verify the unbroken sequence of input or output transactions and take corrective action, should there be a break in sequence. One form of corrective action would be to notify the terminal operator and to close down the transmitting station's ability to transmit data until the remote station takes some sort of corrective action.

2. Have the programs compare the total count of input transactions to a predetermined total count or to a count of output transactions.

3. Let the program perform automated and/or preprogrammed editing for all input after it gets into the computer. Some of the editing that the program can perform might be as follows:

— Count the number of fields in a record and compare that with a predetermined number of fields.

— Check for the reasonableness of the input data with regard to some set of preestablished boundaries.

— Test the data for blanks, sign (plus or minus), numeric, or alphabetic, and compare that with a preestablished criteria.

— Check for consistency between fields of an input transaction (this would be a specific control with regard to a specific application input).

— Conduct a limit test, and reject data or take corrective action whenever the data falls outside of some limit or predetermined range.

— Check for completeness of data, for example, the zip code field should be full, and it should contain numeric data only.

— Conduct sequence checking in order to insure correct sequence.

— Conduct date checking in order to insure that the dates are correct whenever this is applicable.

— Use self-checking numbers that pinpoint erroneous entry of account numbers or whatever type of number the organization is using.

— Enter critical data twice on one transaction input and have the computer programs cross-check these two inputs to insure that, first it was entered correctly, and second there was no error during transmission.

4. Let the computer programs compare or crossfoot predetermined control figures such as:

— Record counts

— Control totals

— Hash totals

— Batch control totals.

5. Have the program recompute various totals of significant financial or accounting figures and transmit these totals back to the original input station.

6. Have the programs prepare specific reports that will display the contents of batch controls, header controls, and any other types of control totals that can be sent back to the original station that inputted the data.

7. Have the programs compare the current data totals with historical totals in order to maintain a logical relationship over time.

8. Have the programs perform logical relationship tests. Logical relationship tests are solely dependent on a specific application because there may be logical relationships within a specific application system.

9. Have the programs look for duplicate entries of data. Whenever duplicate

entries are suspected, the original station inputting the data should be immediately notified.

10. Design systems so upon the discovery of erroneous data during processing, the original entry station is immediately notified so correction can take place as soon as possible.

11. Insure that whenever the program edits an incoming record and it finds an error, it continues editing the entire record to see if there is more than one error. This is to avoid the possibility of the program rejecting an input transaction because of an error, and after correcting that error and reentering the correction into the system finding a second error in the original input. This control reduces the cycling of erroneous input messages.

12. Where feasible, incorporate the editing/validation routines into the remote areas of a distributed or data communication network to reduce transmitting erroneous data.

13. Do not provide users with the capability of overriding computer program edits.

14. Do not allow fall-through comparison tests when editing.

15. Have the system produce a report containing all erroneous transactions and identify the invalid data, out of balance data, and the like.

16. Maintain an opening day transaction count record and a closing day transaction count record. These should be equal and should be compared between the central system and the remote data input stations.

17. Have the programs compare transaction date to the cutoff date table. Transactions entering after the cutoff date should be suspended until after closing. The totals of significant fields of the suspended items are to be reported. These suspended items will not be included in the closing balance because they are for the following period.

18. Insure that the data management program (the scheduler) determines potential conflicts between two users attempting to access the same file and keeps these two separate.

19. See that the data management system can prohibit two programs from simultaneously updating the same record but not the same file.

20. Have the master file update program (especially data management—data base) log the after-image of each data base update. This may not be necessary if the data base is a small one that can be copied over each day.

21. Maintain a file that reflects all updated master records and that can be used to recover from a master file loss.

22. Develop and maintain a formal system to control program changes. This system should control and log the changes to any computer program (application software or operations software).

23. Maintain a program that will control the various computer program libraries and will show whenever modifications have been made to these computer program libraries that reside within the computer.

24. See that there are various tables within the computer programs to validate and verify individual user security codes (passwords), unique terminal identification codes, transaction security codes, and any other type of verification of input data that might be necessary. This verification involves verifying prior to allowing entry to the system.

25. See that there is a cross-correlation between the individual user's security code (password) and the transactions, computer programs, computer systems, or other areas that that individual user is allowed to access.

26. See that there are reporting programs that can be used to identify all transactions entered by a specific user (password).

27. Insure that all transactions are dated, time stamped, and logged immediately upon entry into the system. Output transactions should be handled in a similar way.

28. Retain all input and output transactions on an independent file that is backed up.

29. Whenever computer programs or data are to be copied over to microfiche, insure that the handling and storage procedures for the microfiche at least equal the security and control within the data processing operations.

30. Maintain a special log of all unscheduled or unusual interventions by computer operations personnel. This should include location, date, time, type of intervention, and action taken.

31. Maintain a file of all changes to any security tables. There should be a formal procedure to be followed when changing the "up front" security tables. These are the tables against which the individual users' passwords are compared. All resident tables that require periodic update should be created and maintained external to the system.

32. See that the update program that produces changes to tables also produces a report containing the changes and the corresponding table entry, both before and after the change.

33. Make sure that all table changes receive appropriate authorization external to the system before the change takes place. This should be a written formal approval and it should be reviewed before the change takes place.

34. Restrict the master commands to the computer system to one physical terminal. These master commands should also be restricted to as few computer operators as possible.

35. Have the computer programs accumulate data for a periodic report showing any unauthorized attempts to access the system, special security type programs, the operating system software, restricted "up-front" tables, and the like.

36. Limit computer operator intervention to system and/or port start-up, terminal backup assignments, emergency message broadcasting, system shutdown, communications debugging, and the system or job status reporting.

37. Design application programs so they do not display messages on the system console or accept data from the system console.

38. Establish access restrictions on system utilities and other sensitive programs that might be utilized to manipulate the system.

39. Consider assigning security codes to files (lockwords) to restrict their access to only certain programs and/or users.

40. Utilize disk and tape labels (internal) and check them with the various programs or program modules.

41. Have programs check the position of various computer console switches if there are any.

42. Log all interruptions by computer operations personnel, and especially save the computer console printing log for review by other personnel.

43. Keep a count on the number of program instructions executed, run time, or any other data for sensitive programs. This can be compared periodically with similar data from a prior period to uncover irregularities.

44. Use a check-sum methodology to control or detect unauthorized program changes. A check-sum count on computer programs can be compared with similar data at a later date to determine if a change was made to a program.

45. Immediately write errors, scuttles, or suspense accounts to eliminate computer operator intervention.

46. Consider using a read-after-write option on magnetic recording devices (especially real-time data base updates).

47. Use program software protection keys to safeguard data in memory, on tape, or on disk.

48. Internally store data in the computer and on magnetic tape/disk using cryptographic techniques. This will protect the organization from a computer memory dump.

49. Whenever a "program control" is overridden or bypassed, note the event on an exception report.

50. Consider using a program that compares a controlled duplicate copy of the source/object program with the program currently being used. This is time consuming and probably should only be used on very sensitive programs whether they are application programs or system software programs.

51. Consider including a listing of the job control language with the output to insure that unauthorized programs have not been executed.

52. Consider having the computer operations personnel insert all job control so computer programs cannot illegally execute programs by manipulating the job control on valid jobs.

53. Consider cataloging the job control language cards so it is more difficult to illegally enter unauthorized job control and also to insure fewer errors from erroneous job control.

54. Consider having hardware that carries the parity bit into memory and throughout the entire system to more readily detect hardware memory or parity errors.

55. Consider hardware that has memory protection areas that separate parts of memory through hardware controls rather than software controls.

56. Use tape units that have write-ring protection, parity, and read-after-write.

57. Use disk units that allow file protect areas and read-after-write.

58. Use card readers that read twice and compare before entering the data.

59. Use specially equipped key disk/tape/punches and verifying machines that automatically provide for self-checking numbers (if applicable).

60. Use hardware that has circuit diagnostic routines to detect errors.

61. When using optical readers, insure that they read twice and compare before transmitting the data to the central system.

62. Allow for lower privilege levels for users as contrasted with the operating system. This may be accomplished either through hardware or software, depending on the computer manufacturer.

63. Have the computer programs programmed so they look for a unique identifier such as a transaction code to direct the transaction to the proper portion of the application program for processing.

64. Have all computer-program-generated transactions printed out in a listing and sorted to whatever is appropriate for direct feedback to users. This control provides for the use of computer-program-generated transaction control at the user level.

65. Control computer-program-generated transactions by putting severe limits or other preprogrammed restrictions on them so they cannot exceed certain values. Any transactions that exceed these values are automatically rejected and are printed out on a special report.

66. Control computer-generated transactions by keeping a count of them, and on a daily basis graphing this and comparing it with other co-related variables. As time goes by, the operations personnel will get to know what is a reasonable quantity of computer-generated transactions.

67. Control computer-generated transactions by developing a daily report of the ten largest, ten smallest, average number of, average dollar value per transaction, and any other averages or quantities that make sense with regard to the specific application being run. In this way the users get a feel for the types of and quantities of computer-program-generated transactions in their system.

68. Control computer-generated transactions by building in balance controls between program modules. These balance controls are automated internal cross-checks. Such controls may take the form of reasonableness checks, who entered the transactions, program-to-program control totals, and the like.

69. Have control totals passed between jobs and job steps during the running of on-line programs. A system of automated controls should include balancing of the entire system as well as balancing between different program modules and/or the final file (data base) control totals.

70. Consider developing default tables for computer programs that have numer-

ous options. This is where a program has several decisions and there is a standardized action for most of or all of these decisions. When developing a default table, make sure that one of the options is to report that none of the options fits the specific situation at hand.

71. Consider anticipation controls. These controls are used as a method of insuring accountability of input. Sequence-checking is a common example of such a control, but the general thought here is to have the programs anticipate what might be coming next.

72. Consider having the computer hardware use techniques such as double arithmetic, arithmetic overflow checks, and reverse multiplication. These checks would only be used at very critical points in the application program calculations.

73. Insure that programs perform a file completion check to determine that the application file has been completely processed and includes all transactions and all items on a master file.

74. See that programs balance computer files and/or data base record changes. The number of records on the opening of a file should be balanced against the changes made during the day and the closing balance. On a regular basis the total of the detail records might be compared to the total in the control records.

75. See that erroneous data is written out to an error file and returned to the user as soon as possible (preferably immediately for immediate correction). Dummy records should never be used to hold erroneous data.

76. Have a specific set of computer operator instructions developed and in use for each application program.

77. Use computer program run books for the specifics of each application program. These would cover items such as console message instructions, error message instructions, program halts, rerun procedures, check-point and restart instructions, check-point control totals, job control setup, and the like.

78. See that the information on error reports indicates all data fields that are in error in a transaction or record.

79. Maintain an automated error suspense file that includes all rejected transactions. These files should be used for follow-up and to correct and reenter the transactions. These files should be aged so it is evident when certain data has not been corrected and reentered.

80. Issue special discrepancy reports to insure that the handling of errors results in their correction and reentry in a timely manner.

81. Automatically assign unique serial numbers to transactions entered into the automated error suspense files. Such serial numbers are used to control subsequent updating or correction of or reentry of the data that was in error.

82. Never allow destructive updates to correct error conditions without first logging both the before and after image of the update. Debit and credit type entries should never be deleted or erased. Debit and credit type of entries should be corrected by instituting the opposite debit and credit rather than deleting or erasing.

83. Insure that there is an automatic program to reenter erroneous data and to correct the error suspense listing so it is brought up to date in a timely fashion.

84. See that computer operations personnel are rotated between various job functions periodically, and that there is a segregation of duties, within reasonable limits, within large data processing operations facilities.

85. Have signature authorizations thoroughly checked with regard to the external formal paperwork approvals that are required for program changes and special runs and other items that are out of the ordinary.

86. Keep both source and object copies of programs (applications and systems) under secure custody so they cannot be easily removed from the organization. The same is true for various historical records whether they reside on magnetic tapes or in data base systems.

87. Test the default options of vendor-supplied operating system software to determine what would happen if the default option itself failed.

88. Be sure that all programs, application programs, and vendor-supplied operating system programs are adequately documented.

89. Have computer programs conduct an overflow check on all numeric fields for which there could be a data overflow.

90. Insure that any fictitious branches or other fictitious entities that are incorporated into the on-line programs for testing or other training purposes are adequately separated from the "real" records and/or computer programs. Insure that these systems cannot contribute to errors and omissions, fraud, or any other serious types of problems such as disasters, system crashes, and the like.

91. Insure that there are adequate manual controls to duly record whenever computer operations personnel are called in at odd times or for an emergency.

92. Downline load new programs to distributed computer sites periodically to insure program code integrity.

OUTPUT CONTROL MATRIX

This chapter defines the control review matrix that might be used when reviewing the output controls of a computerized system. The controls listed in this matrix are specifically designed to control the outputs from the computer system (these controls may be utilized with both on-line systems and batch systems). These output controls may be interrelated with the input controls, chapter 3; program/computer processing controls, chapter 5; and the on-line terminal controls, chapter 7.

THE MATRIX APPROACH

The internal control area to be reviewed using this matrix covers outputs from the computer system. These outputs may be directly affected by input controls, program/computer processing controls, and on-line terminal controls. When reviewing the output controls, match each resource/asset with its corresponding concern/exposure as listed in Figure 6-1: Output Control Matrix. This matrix lists the resources in relation to the potential exposures and cross-relates these with the various controls/safeguards that should be considered when reviewing the outputs from computer systems (see chapter 1 for an explanation on how to use the control matrix approach).

Immediately following the matrix is a definition of each of the concerns/exposures that are listed across the top of the matrix and each of the resources/assets that are listed down the left vertical column of the matrix. Following these definitions is a complete numerical listing and description of each of the controls/safeguards that are listed numerically in the cells of the matrix.

CONCERNS/EXPOSURES

The following concerns/exposures are those that are directly applicable to the outputs of an on-line or batch type of computerized system. The definition for each of these exposures, listed across the top of the matrix, is as follows:

- Output Balancing and Reconciliation—The responsibility for the monitoring of data processing related controls. This concern sometimes manifests itself as a quality assurance function within the data processing department, insuring that the integrity of the data has not been lost during the data processing cycle.

- Privacy—The accidental or intentional release of data about an individual, assuming that the release of this personal information was improper to the normal conduct of the business at the organization.

CONCERNS / EXPOSURES

RESOURCES / ASSETS

	OUTPUT BALANCING AND RECON-CILIATION	PRIVACY	SECURITY/ THEFT	OUTPUT DISTRIBUTION	USER BALANCING AND RECON-CILIATION	RECORDS RETENTION AND DESTRUCTION	NEGOTIABLE DOCUMENTS	OUTPUT ERROR HANDLING		
OUTPUT DEVICES	9, 31-34, 41	9	9, 31, 33	9, 25, 34	41			9, 27, 31, 41		
PEOPLE	1-3,8,9,11,12, 14, 16, 28, 30 31, 36-38	4-6, 14	4-6, 14, 21, 37	1,4,6,10,12-15, 17, 21, 30, 34	1, 2, 4, 8, 11, 27, 28, 36, 37	5, 7, 10, 15, 19, 26, 35, 43	5, 7, 20-23, 43	3, 8, 16, 27-31, 36-38		
RECORDS STORAGE AND DISPOSAL		7, 43	7, 37, 43			5, 7, 15, 19, 26, 35, 43	5, 7, 43	35, 39		
OPERATIONAL PROCEDURES	1-3, 8,9, 11, 12, 14, 16, 28-34, 36-42	4-7, 14, 18, 19, 24	4-7, 14, 18, 19, 21, 24, 33, 37, 40	1,4,6,10,12-17, 21, 24, 30, 34	1, 2, 4, 8, 11, 27-29, 36, 37, 40, 41	7, 10, 19, 26, 35, 43	20-23, 43	3, 8, 16,27-30, 36-41		

FIGURE 6-1: OUTPUT CONTROL MATRIX

- Security/Theft—The security or theft of information that should have been kept confidential because of its proprietary nature. In a way, this is a form of privacy, but the information removed from the organization does not pertain to an individual. The information might be inadvertently (accidentally) released, or it might be the subject of an outright theft. This exposure also includes the theft of assets such as might be experienced in embezzlement, fraud, or defalcation.

- Output Distribution—A review to insure the delivery of complete and accurate reports to the authorized recipients in a timely manner.

- User Balancing and Reconciliation—Insurance that the integrity of the data has not been lost during the processing by the application system. This concern involves the final users' reviewing, scanning, balancing, and reconciling the data that they have received.

- Records Retention and Destruction—The controls that are used to guide the retention and disposal of confidential or private computer system output. In this context, the disposal may be immediate, or it might come after some years of retaining computer output. This concern should include both paper documents, magnetic media, and microforms.

- Negotiable Documents—The handling of negotiable documents (blank check stock, etc.) and prevention of their loss. This concern may also involve accountable documents which are not negotiable, but whose loss would be injurious to the organization.

- Output Error Handling—The procedures and methods used to insure that all transactions rejected during the system processing are corrected and reentered. The object here is to insure that any output documents found to be in error are corrected.

RESOURCES/ASSETS

The following resources/assets are those that should be reviewed during the output control review. The definition for each of these assets, listed down the left vertical column of the matrix, is as follows:

- Output Devices—The peripheral devices connected to the central computer system (also including the computer itself) and the types of errors that might be made by this hardware. The output devices for any controls, their current usage, operational procedures, and any written documentation pertaining to them should be reviewed.

- People—The individuals responsible for reconciling the output data, operating and maintaining the output devices, writing operational procedures, and managing the output quality assurance function. This may also include user department personnel.

- Records Storage and Disposal—The storage of output data (hard copy or microform) as well as the disposal of this data. This includes reviewing the storage area and the disposal techniques.

- Operational Procedures—The written operational procedures on how to obtain data, verification, reconciliation, and those other aspects of delivering output data from data processing (whether it is centralized or distributed) to the various users.

CONTROLS/SAFEGUARDS

The following controls/safeguards should be considered when reviewing the outputs of an on-line or batch type of computerized system. This numerical listing describes each control.

It should be noted that implementation of various controls can be both costly and time consuming. It is of great importance that a realistic and pragmatic evaluation be made with regard to the probability of a specific exposure affecting a specific asset. Only then can the control for safeguarding the asset be evaluated in a cost-effective manner.

The controls, as numerically listed in the cells of the matrix, are as follows:

1. Visually scan output reports for completeness and proper formatting.

2. On a random basis, thoroughly check a specific output report for correctness.

3. Always review all errors and the reason for these errors in order to determine if there is a program bug or input problem.

4. Control the distribution of reports so they are sent only to the proper and authorized personnel.

5. Keep all sensitive reports in a secure area so unauthorized personnel cannot obtain copies.

6. Verify that the current handling procedures for output reports are being followed.

7. Immediately destroy aborted output runs (paper shredder) for sensitive outputs.

8. Print out computer-generated control totals and cross-relate these back to the manually inputted control totals, for example, verify record counts, hash totals, batch totals, and the like.

9. Periodically review computer console error messages and system output error messages to try to determine if there are program bugs.

10. Institute an overall report analysis program to determine whether any reports can be eliminated, combined, rearranged, simplified, or whether new reports may be required.

11. Manually maintain an output log of expected results and compare the actual output to the expected output.

12. Consider developing an independent control group within the data processing function that is responsible for the quality control of output reports.

13. Maintain a job schedule desk with appropriate cutoff times so it can be determined when jobs are to be run and so the output control group can insure timely report delivery.

14. Determine the number of output documents received and insure that it agrees with the number of documents the program reported as producing. This may manifest itself as a page count routine.

15. Try to include the following elements in the heading of each report: date prepared, processing period covered, a descriptive title of the report contents, the user department, the processing program's identification job number, how to dispose of the report, and its confidentiality.

16. Number the pages consecutively, and indicate that the report came to a normal ending with a positive statement as to such.

17. Label the cover of all reports to indicate the recipient's name and location.

18. Identify any confidential reports as being confidential and proprietary information.

19. Label any reports that must be positively and completely destroyed as to their disposal procedures. In other words, a report that should be returned to a central destruction area should be labeled as such, or it should be labeled to be destroyed in a paper shredder or whatever.

20. At regular intervals, take an inventory of any prenumbered negotiable documents.

21. Consider having a processing program print an additional sequence number on prenumbered forms. The differences between the beginning and ending preprinted number and the beginning and ending of the computer-generated number must agree. The output control group should reconcile these two numbers.

22. Maintain all negotiable documents in a secure location and control access to this location.

23. Maintain signature stamps (such as for payroll) in a different physical location from the negotiable documents themselves.

24. Produce only the required number of output reports.

25. Clearly describe in the operations procedures manual what type of paper stock and/or forms should be used in the print devices.

26. Consider filing output reports by date so at the end of a calendar year they can be discarded when their retention date has been reached.

27. When reviewing output reports that are in error, indicate all data fields in error on the report, and submit them to the programming department for possible evaluation and correction of programs.

28. Produce control totals for all rejects and pass these control totals back to the input area for correction and reentry.

29. Clearly define in the operations procedures manual the procedures for error correction and reentry responsibility.

30. The output control totals for each application should be reconciled with the input totals before the release of the output report from the data processing to the user department.

31. Compare any transaction log maintained by the computer system with a transaction log maintained at each output device. These totals should be

verified against individual application control totals established at other steps in the processing stream to verify that everything has been properly processed to its final step.

32. In order to monitor process flow, maintain a record that indicates the average time between the input of user data and the actual starting of each application run. One of the sources that might be used for this purpose is the automatic job accounting routines in some vendors' system software.

33. Develop and review an automated job accounting system. This type of control can be utilized to review the time utilized to process jobs, which files and/or programs were used by the jobs, the time it took to print jobs, and other valuable pieces of information. Vendors' accounting record job routines (for example, IBM has Systems Management Facilities) can be utilized for many unique output control tasks.

34. Consider reviewing the job control used for specific jobs whenever there is a discrepancy in the output.

35. Insure that there are appropriate waste disposal procedures for the immediate disposal of certain paper products (sensitive output reports).

36. Consider obtaining a list of all transactions that went into a specific report whenever there are discrepancies.

37. Consider maintaining an independent history file of errors, which is independent of all processing files, and is regularly analyzed to report error trends and statistics by type, source, and frequency of errors within an application system.

38. Insure that all data rejected from a processing cycle of an application is entered in an error log by a control group. This log is then used to insure the correction and reentry of data.

39. Insure that error correction procedures are defined in the operations procedures manual.

40. Insure that header and trailer labels/record counts are printed out at the end of each output report.

41. Even though some on-line systems are individual transaction oriented, consider having the remote terminal operators enter their data in small batches of two to ten transactions.

42. Insure that lengthy output reports have checkpoint and restart capabilities so an entire report need not be printed if there was an error near its end. In this way, the outputting of this report can go back to a prior partition and all the processing time is not lost.

43. When decollating a sensitive job, insure that the carbon paper is disposed of in a secure manner.

ON-LINE TERMINAL/DISTRIBUTED SYSTEMS CONTROL MATRIX

7

This chapter outlines the control review matrix that might be used when reviewing the remote terminals of an on-line system (especially distributed systems). The controls/safeguards listed in this matrix are specifically designed for on-line systems. If the EDP auditor is reviewing batch-oriented systems, then the input control matrix of chapter 3 should also be utilized.

THE MATRIX APPROACH

The internal control area to be reviewed using this matrix covers on-line terminal/ distributed systems controls. These on-line system controls involve those controls that should be considered when using terminals as input or output devices to an on-line system. When reviewing the on-line terminal/distributed systems controls, match each resource/asset with its corresponding concern/exposure as listed in Figure 7-1: On-Line Terminal/Distributed Systems Control Matrix. This matrix lists the resources in relation to the potential exposures and cross-relates these with the various controls/ safeguards that should be considered when reviewing the on-line terminal/distributed systems controls (see chapter 1 for an explanation on how to use the control matrix approach).

Immediately following the matrix is a definition of each of the concerns/exposures that are listed across the top of the matrix and each of the resources/assets that are listed down the left vertical column of the matrix. Following these definitions is a complete numerical listing and description of each of the controls/safeguards that are listed numerically in the cells of the matrix.

CONCERNS/EXPOSURES

The following concerns/exposures are those that are directly applicable to the remote terminal stations of an on-line system (especially distributed systems). The definition for each of these exposures, listed across the top of the matrix, is as follows:

- Errors and Omissions—The accidental or intentional inputting of data that is in error, including the accidental or intentional omission of data that should have been entered into the on-line system. This type of exposure includes, but is not limited to, inaccurate data, incomplete data, malfunctioning terminals, and the like.

- Disasters and Disruptions (natural and man-made)—The temporary or long-term disruption of normal data processing capabilities. This exposure renders the organization's normal processing capabilities inoperative.

- Privacy—The accidental or intentional release of data about an individual, assuming that the release of this personal information was improper to the normal conduct of business at the organization.

CONCERNS / EXPOSURES

RESOURCES / ASSETS

	ERRORS AND OMISSIONS	DISASTERS AND DISRUPTIONS	PRIVACY	SECURITY/ THEFT	HUMAN ERROR PREVENTION	MESSAGE LOSS OR CHANGE	ILLEGAL PENE- TRATION	TERMINAL DATA ENTRY AND VALIDATION	TRANS- ACTION ENTRY ERROR HANDLING	
TERMINALS	20,21,37,41,44 46-50,53-56, 63	3, 8, 24, 30, 36, 39, 58, 59	1,4,6-11,13,15, 17, 19, 22, 34, 40, 51, 52, 60, 68	1,4,6-11,13,15, 17, 19, 22, 34, 40, 51, 52, 60, 61, 68	37, 41, 43, 46-50, 53-56, 63, 64-67	19-22, 27-29,	4,6-11,13,15, 17, 19, 22, 24, 30, 34, 40, 51, 52, 60, 68	1,37,41,44,47, 49, 53, 54, 56, 60, 63	55-57, 61, 63,	
DISTRIBUTED INTELLIGENCE	20,21,37,41, 43-50,53-56, 63	3, 24, 30, 32, 33, 35, 36, 39, 58, 59	4-6,8-19,22, 23,25,26,30-34, 40,51,52,60,62, 68	4-6,8-19,22,23, 25,26,30-34,40, 51,52,60,61,68	37,38,43,45-50, 53-56,63-66	19-22, 25-29, 32-34	4-6, 8-19, 22-26, 30-34, 40, 51, 52, 60, 62, 68	1, 41, 47, 49, 53, 54, 56, 60, 62, 63	53, 55-57, 63	
PEOPLE	43-50, 53-56, 63, 66	2, 24, 33	2, 4, 6-16, 18, 23, 25, 26, 33, 34, 40, 42, 43, 51, 52, 60, 62	2, 4, 6-16, 18, 23, 25, 26, 31, 33, 34, 40, 42, 43, 51, 52, 60-62	25, 43-50, 53-56, 63-67	25, 26, 28, 29	2, 4-16, 18, 23, 25,26,30,31-34, 40, 42, 51, 52, 60, 62	1, 25-29, 37, 43, 44, 47, 49, 53, 54, 56, 60, 63-65	55-57, 61, 63	
CENTRAL SYSTEM	37, 44-48, 50, 55, 56, 63	3,24,30,32,33, 35, 36, 39	4-6, 8-18,22, 23, 25, 26, 30-34, 40, 51, 52, 60, 62, 68	4-6, 8-18, 22, 23,25,26,30-34, 40,51,52,60,61, 62, 68	37, 38, 43, 45-48, 50, 55, 56, 63-66	19, 21, 25-29, 32-34, 36	4-6,8-18,22-26, 30-34,36,40,51, 52, 60, 62, 68	1, 37, 47, 54, 56, 60, 62, 63	55-57, 63	

FIGURE 7-1: ON-LINE TERMINAL/DISTRIBUTED SYSTEMS CONTROL MATRIX

- Security/Theft—The security or theft of information that should have been kept confidential because of its proprietary nature. In a way, this is a form of privacy, but the information removed from the organization does not pertain to an individual. The information might be inadvertently (accidentally) released, or it might be the subject of an outright theft. This exposure also includes the theft of assets such as might be experienced in embezzlement, fraud, or defalcation.

- Human Error Prevention—Reduction of the number of errors made by human beings during their input to or use of the remote terminals.

- Message Loss or Change—The loss of a message or its inadvertent change after it was entered at the remote on-line terminal.

- Illegal Penetration—Insure that only the proper and authorized personnel utilize the system.

- Terminal Data Entry and Validation—The entry of data at the remote site, data entry error-checking procedures, and the validation of data at the remote site by an intelligent type device (distributed systems).

- Transaction Entry Error Handling—The methodologies and controls for handling errors at the remote site prior to transmitting them to the centralized computer system. This may also involve the error-handling procedures of a distributed data processing system (at the distributed site).

RESOURCES/ASSETS

The following resources/assets are those that should be reviewed during the on-line terminal (distributed systems) control review. The definition for each of these assets, listed down the left vertical column of the matrix, is as follows:

- Terminals—Any or all of the input or output devices used to interconnect with the on-line system. This resource would specifically include, without excluding other devices, teleprinter terminals, video terminals, remote job entry terminals, transaction terminals, intelligent terminals, and other devices used with distributed systems. These may also include microprocessors or minicomputers (when they are the input or output device), and disk or tape units.

- Distributed Intelligence—The provision for or capability for error detection and/or correction, authentication, message formatting, data validation, check sums, protocol, and any other logical or arithmetic function for validating the integrity of data transmitted from the terminal. This type of distributed intelligence is very prevalent in distributed data processing systems, but it might also reside in an intelligent terminal or at a common carrier's switch if the common carrier offers a concentration function or a packet-switching function.

- People—The individuals responsible for inputting data, operating and maintaining the equipment, writing the programs, and managing the remote terminals and/or the distributed system.

- Central System—Most prevalent in the form of a central computer to which the terminal transmits and receives, but in a fully distributed system with equal processing at each distributed node, there might not be an identifiable central system (just some other identifiable equal distributed systems).

CONTROLS/SAFEGUARDS

The following controls/safeguards should be considered when reviewing the remote terminal stations of an on-line system (especially distributed systems). This numerical listing describes each control.

It should be noted that implementation of various controls can be both costly and time consuming. It is of great importance that a realistic and pragmatic evaluation be made with regard to the probability of a specific exposure affecting a specific asset. Only then can the control for safeguarding the asset be evaluated in a cost-effective manner.

The controls, as numerically listed in the cells of the matrix, are as follows:

1. Have a general policy pertaining to the on-line terminal requirements and the uses to which these on-line terminals may be put.

2. Insure that employees in sensitive positions are subject to special controls and especially a thorough review upon hiring.

3. Review the insurance coverage with regard to the remote terminals and remote distributed processing sites.

4. Consider transaction coding the terminals so only certain application system transactions can be entered from certain terminals. In this way the use to which a terminal may be put by its location within a specific work area can be restricted.

5. Consider using a departmental user number. This departmental user number is a "type of" security control although it is known to all members of a specific department (it is primarily a number used for billing purposes).

6. Utilize an individual security code called a password. The password is a secret number known only to one individual user, and it must be kept confidential. Passwords can be cross-related to terminal identification schemes and to application transactions for which the user is authorized. Insure that passwords are changed at various times and that the passwords of employees who leave the organization are immediately removed from the system. Also insure whenever a central authority issues passwords that they are truly random, that they are printed and distributed in a secure fashion, and that adequate measures are taken for their timely reissuance. If the organization allows the users to develop their own passwords, insure that there is a computer program to review each new password to see that it is unique and that it is not just a copy of the user's name, four or more similar characters, or some other combination that is easily discernible. One further point would be to insure that the number of actual passwords being utilized is at a ratio of approximately 1 to 200 with regard to the number of passwords available (in other words, if there were 10,000 available passwords, be sure that no more than 50 are actually assigned).

7. Keep the remote terminals in a physically secure location so only authorized personnel can actually utilize the terminals.

8. Obtain terminals with lockable keyboards that can be locked up from the remote computer site or distributed intelligence in case the central control function desires to shut down a terminal.

9. Insure that the terminals have a nonprinting feature for use when keying in the individual security code (password) so it cannot be seen by personnel in the area.

10. As an alternative to individual security codes (passwords) consider an identification card reader that would read the employee's badge, or fingerprint detectors, handprint detectors, voice detection, or signature verification. The current state of the art and the current acceptance of the method by the public at large tends to lean toward signature verification as a personal identification device.

11. Even though terminals may be in a physically secure location, consider putting a physical keylock on the terminal's on/off switch. In this way, when the authorized operator leaves the terminal, it can be locked.

12. Insure that the communication facilities, when they are shut down, are locked off in an inoperative state. This insures that the terminal operator cannot gain illegal entry into the system during off-hours.

13. With regard to logging-in a terminal, consider special log-in passwords (separate from the individual operator's password) that will be transmitted from the terminal to the central site or distributed intelligence for verification. Also consider having the central site or distributed intelligence send some sort of identifier back to the terminal operator.

14. Restrict some terminals to input only, output only, or both input and output, as is appropriate with regard to the business application.

15. Restrict some terminals to the type of message that can be sent or received to or from the terminal.

16. Cross-relate the individual security code (user password) to the type of transactions that are authorized by this individual. In this way, an individual can be limited to the type of transactions for which he or she is authorized. This is a form of "electronic separation of duties" which can be very effective in restricting transactions that should be separated between different personnel.

17. Correlate the circuit identification (identification of the communication line) to the physical terminals or individual security codes that would be coming in on that specific communication circuit. This is another form of cross-relating an individual security code to areas where this security code is authorized.

18. When the terminal is allowed direct dial access into the central system or distributed intelligence, consider some of the following controls: keep the telephone numbers secret and change the telephone numbers periodically; when the terminal operator dials in, have someone at the central site or distributed intelligence point make a verbal indentification of the caller; have the central site or distributed intelligence record the caller's password and then return the call to the caller (in this way, the central site or distributed intelligence controls to whom they will return calls).

19. Sequence number all messages, both inbound and outbound, starting with message number 1 each day. In this way, lost messages can be identified, as well as illegal messages in the message stream to or from the terminal.

20. Consider logging (safe store) all messages at the remote terminal.

21. Acknowledge receipt of all messages, either by the central site or distributed intelligence and by the remote terminal itself.

22. Use some sort of encryption or secret test keys to protect sensitive data within messages.

23. Protect the privacy and secrecy of passwords and log-in codes.

24. Whenever dial-up backup communication facilities are used, have the central site or distributed intelligence check to insure that the private leased communication facilities have, in fact, failed.

25. Consider special control reports for terminal security and password security such as the number of log-ins or log-outs (especially unsuccessful log-ins), the sequence number errors in the message stream (report these immediately to the sending terminal, and log it out), the number of unusual log-outs and where they took place, all alterations of previously entered messages, any messages left in the system at system shutdown, and the like.

26. Consider some on-line daily reports such as the current message status by terminal, message delivery criteria, the current log-in/log-out status of all terminals and all individual security codes (passwords), all undelivered messages, total message count (both inbound and outbound) by terminals, and the like.

27. On very large systems, utilize a message priority structure for efficiency to insure that the most important messages get delivered.

28. Insure that there are message tracing routines (audit trail) so a terminal user can trace a message once he or she has sent it.

29. Insure that there are message retrieval routines (audit trail) so a terminal user can retrieve prior messages that have been sent.

30. For distributed intelligence systems, consider downline loading programs to the remote stations such as concentrators, intelligent terminals, and the like. In this way, a program can be changed at various times of the day and especially after maintenance has been performed to downline equipment.

31. Consider taking check-sum counts at various times during the day to insure that the downline programs have not been modified.

32. Journalize all system commands entered through the system control console so they can be reviewed at a later date. Consider putting these onto microfiche.

33. Stringently control circuit test equipment. This specifically covers network monitoring equipment with which to read the data going over the comunication lines. It is even more important to stringently control the programmable network monitoring equipment. This equipment is necessary although the personnel authorized to use it should be limited. The uses to which it should be put should clearly be stated, and it should be locked up in some fashion when it is not in use (this locking up might involve removing it from the area, installing a keylock switch in place of the on/off switch, or covering it with a lockable metal hood so it is unusable).

34. Review the software controls at remote intelligent devices with regard to protection against unauthorized access, message accountability, and procedures for the control of software changes as well as data base administration (especially with distributed systems).

35. Review the various modes of restart for distributed intelligence. This may range from a cold start to a fully automated recovery.

36. Review hardware controls on distributed systems such as software memory protection, disk file protection, read after write, hardware types of memory protection, time-sharing operations software control procedures, dial-up modems, and the like.

37. Review the operator manuals to insure that they are thorough and up to date.

38. Review the software documentation with regard to distributed systems (especially distributed intelligence).

39. Review contingency planning at remote distributed system sites such as contingency planning for total disaster, bomb threat, fire, partial disaster, and the like.

40. Review the disposal of "sensitive" documents at remote terminal sites.

41. Review the training plan for the operations personnel with regard to the remote terminal sites and distributed systems.

42. Insure that user handbooks, operations manuals, software documentation, and other such items are marked as personal and private confidential information belonging to the specific organization involved. Also, insure that they specify how to dispose of unneeded copies.

43. Insure that adequate operator training is provided and that there are operator manuals which are updated periodically.

44. Try to insure that there is a simple dialog between the operator and the application system. A simple dialog with a straightforward keyboard usually results in fewer errors upon input.

45. Preprogram instructions on how to use the system into the system and have them available for recall whenever an operator needs them (this will reduce the number of human errors on input).

46. Insure that there are restart procedures and checkpoints for terminal operators to use during a complicated input transaction.

47. Design the system with format aids such as preselected formats to work the operator through the system in an orderly manner, or preprinted forms or menu selection format techniques, and the like. This will result in fewer operator errors.

48. Provide an adequate work area for operators with regard to light, noise, temperature, and the like. To reduce operator boredom, try to insure a reasonably fast response time (two to four seconds), utilize graphics, color, flashing elements, varying character size, broken lines, and any other methods that will reduce errors upon input.

49. Consider using distributed intelligence to edit and verify the data prior

to transmission to the central site or distributed system itself.

50. Consider computer-aided instruction in order to reduce the number of operator errors and as a method of training new operators.

51. Forbid master commands to be entered from a remote terminal. Master commands are those that change basic system parameters or affect operational programs or data bases. These should only be allowed from the central master console.

52. Periodically review the assignment and priority levels of individual security codes (passwords), terminal priorities, terminal identification circuits, circuit identifications, and the like.

53. Perform editing and validating routines at the distributed intelligence or remote terminal points.

54. Immediately return erroneous data to the terminal operators so they can correct it on-line.

55. Develop listings for erroneous data and use these to insure that the entries have been corrected and reentered into the system. Consider having this be an on-line file that would operate in a real-time fashion.

56. When reentering data (corrected data), insure that the corrected data editing is done by using the same rules and/or programs as for processing the original transaction. It is best to resubmit the entire transaction.

57. Have control totals produced for all rejects. These totals should reflect new rejects as well as the elimination of accepted data. Reconciliation of these control totals may be accomplished through manual monitoring of the data resubmission or through the use of a computer control program using suspense file principles.

58. Consider backup hardware for remote terminal sites (this depends upon the criticality of the business operation).

59. Review the preventive maintenance for the hardware at distributed sites (this should be both available and quick).

60. Where appropriate and necessary, make sure the user verifies authorization of inputs, either through the use of a signature on a source document, a user password, or some other method of authorization.

61. Where feasible, segregate the functions of the generation of the transaction, the input of the transaction (on-line terminal input), and the custody of the assets. This may not be practical in an on-line system that has no source documents.

62. When logging input transactions, include the terminal identification and user password for audit trail purposes.

63. Even though this is a review of an on-line system, consider using variable size batches when large quantities of similar data are being inputted into the system. These batches would be internally accumulated and cross-checked with the batch numbers that are inputted by the terminal operator.

64. Try to include both business date and data processing date as a field in a transaction.

65. Consider using the Julian date as a part of the transaction number.

66. Publish processing cycles to allow users to control their cutoff dates. Have the computerized system check for cutoff dates to insure timely entry of transactions.

67. Instruct terminal operators to utilize scanning techniques or sight verification prior to transmitting messages.

68. Utilize a unique terminal identification chip. This is a circuit chip built in to the terminal so whenever the terminal is logged in, the central site or distributed intelligence interrogates the terminal to get its identification. In this way, the organization can control which terminals will be allowed to interconnect with the central or distributed system.

PHYSICAL SECURITY CONTROL MATRIX

This chapter defines and discusses the control review matrix that might be used when conducting a physical security review of the data processing organization. The controls/safeguards listed in this matrix are specifically designed for reviewing the physical security and control of the data processing function.

THE MATRIX APPROACH

The internal control area to be reviewed using this matrix covers physical security of the data processing function. Physical security may involve the computer operations, computer programming, systems development, and all other associated aspects of the overall data processing function. When reviewing the physical security controls, match each resource/asset with its corresponding concern/exposure as listed in Figure 8-1: Physical Security Control Matrix. This matrix lists the resources in relation to the potential exposures and cross-relates these with the various controls/safeguards that should be considered when reviewing physical security (see chapter 1 for an explanation on how to use the control matrix approach).

Immediately following the matrix is a definition of each of the concerns/exposures that are listed across the top of the matrix and each of the resources/assets that are listed down the left vertical column of the matrix. Following these definitions is a complete numerical listing and description of each of the controls/safeguards that are listed numerically in the cells of the matrix.

CONCERNS/EXPOSURES

The following concerns/exposures are those that are directly applicable to the review of the physical security of the data processing function. The definition for each of these exposures, listed across the top of the matrix, is as follows:

- Access Control—Control of the access of individuals into and out of the data processing facility. This concern may involve allowing some individuals to have access to certain areas and others to have access to all areas of the data processing facility.

- Security/Theft—The security or theft of information, hardware, and software that should have been kept confidential because of its proprietary nature. In a way, this is a form of privacy, but the information removed from the organization does not pertain to an individual. The information might be inadvertently (accidentally) released, or it might be the subject of an outright theft. This exposure also includes the theft of assets such as might be experienced in embezzlement, fraud, or defalcation.

- Privacy—The accidental or intentional release of data about an individual, assuming that the release of this personal information was improper to the normal conduct of the business at the organization.

- Disaster and Disruption—The major interruption of the continued use of the data processing facility. This concern would include both the intentional or unintentional destruction or partial destruction (fire, flood, etc.) of the data processing facility, so it could not operate in its normal fashion.

- Interrupted Processing—A temporary or short-term interruption of the data processing facility. This may not involve a disastrous situation, but only a temporary disruption of maybe a few minutes or hours.

- Storage and Disposal—The exposures that might culminate from inadequate short- or long-term storage of data, including the proper disposal of data or information after its useful life has expired.

RESOURCES/ASSETS

The following resources/assets are those that should be reviewed during the physical security control review. The definition for each of these assets, listed down the left vertical column of the matrix, is as follows:

- Management Attitude—The overall attitude of the management with regard to security at the various levels in and around the data processing facility.

- Facility Construction—The construction of the facility surrounding the data processing resource and the various internal components of that facility which, when taken collectively, integrate into a smooth-flowing and secure data processing operation.

- Electrical and Motor Generators—The electrical supply for the data processing operations (a loss of electricity may cripple the data processing operations) including special generators.

- Air-Conditioning and Chilled Water—The cooling capabilities for the computer system. As is well known, a loss of cooling can temporarily or permanently cripple the data processing operations.

- Contingency Planning—The plans and testing of the plans that will go into effect should there be a major disaster or disruption, or a temporary interruption to the processing.

- Training Programs—The continuous ongoing training for employees in security and confidentiality.

- People—The individuals responsible for data processing operations, programming, systems development, and any other operations that are performed during development and running of the computerized system.

- Insurance—The insurance that might be carried to compensate the organization should a major disaster or some other perturbation occur.

CONTROLS/SAFEGUARDS

The following controls/safeguards should be considered when reviewing the physical security of the data processing function. This numerical listing describes each control.

It should be noted that implementation of various controls can be both costly and time consuming. It is of great importance that a realistic and pragmatic evaluation be made with regard to the probability of a specific exposure affecting a specific asset. Only then can the control for safeguarding the asset be evaluated in a cost-effective manner.

CONCERNS / EXPOSURES

RESOURCES / ASSETS

RESOURCES / ASSETS	ACCESS CONTROL	SECURITY/ THEFT	PRIVACY	DISASTER AND DISRUPTION	INTER-RUPTED PROCESSING	STORAGE AND DISPOSAL				
MANAGEMENT ATTITUDE	43, 66, 70-72, 74, 76-78, 80-83, 87, 93-95, 97, 100	70, 79, 81, 83, 87, 94-97, 100, 101	70, 81, 83, 87, 94-97, 100, 101	24, 27, 30, 31, 35, 46, 50, 87, 90, 95	24, 27, 30, 31, 35, 46, 50, 86, 87, 90, 95	82, 83, 87, 89, 91, 92				
FACILITY CONSTRUCTION	3-5, 7, 8, 13, 53, 62, 70-73, 96-99	3-5, 7, 13, 53, 62, 70-73, 96, 97	3, 4, 53, 62, 70-73, 96, 97	1, 2, 5, 6, 8, 10, 11, 13-19, 22, 25, 26, 28, 29, 37, 39-41, 45, 51, 61-63, 65, 71, 82, 99	1, 2, 5, 6, 8, 10-20, 22, 23, 25, 26, 28, 29, 37, 39-41, 45 51, 61-63, 65, 71, 98, 99	6, 8-11, 14, 21, 27, 91, 92				
ELECTRICAL AND MOTOR GENERATORS	38, 42, 43, 54, 56, 57, 60			30, 33-37, 39-46, 54, 55, 60, 62	30, 33-37, 39-46, 54, 55, 60, 62					
AIR CONDITIONING AND CHILLED WATER	57			30, 37, 47-59, 61, 62	30, 37, 47-59, 61, 62	47				
CONTINGENCY PLANNING	67, 68, 73, 96-99	88	88	63, 64, 69, 88, 90	63, 64, 69, 86, 88, 90	87-91				
TRAINING PROGRAMS	66, 68, 70, 72, 74, 82, 84, 85, 94, 96	84, 85	84, 85	32, 67, 82, 85, 94	32, 67, 85, 94	94				
PEOPLE	62, 66, 67, 70-72, 74, 75, 78, 80, 81, 83, 94, 97, 98, 100	62, 70, 79, 81, 91, 94, 100, 101	71, 81, 91, 94, 100	23, 30, 31, 36, 63, 66, 67, 69, 90, 98	23, 24, 30, 31, 36, 63, 66, 67, 90, 98	89, 91, 92				
INSURANCE				102-108	102 -108	102, 106				

FIGURE 8-1: PHYSICAL SECURITY CONTROL MATRIX

The controls, as numerically listed in the cells of the matrix, are as follows:

1. Determine whether the building's construction, including walls, roof, and floors, are of noncombustible materials in order to reduce the chance of fire.

2. See that walls immediately adjacent to critical equipment or media are of masonry so they cannot be easily penetrated.

3. See that walls extend from the building's structural floor to the building's structural ceiling and not from raised floors to lowered ceilings in order to stop surreptitious entry to sensitive computer areas.

4. Physically separate the computer facility from other departments.

5. In multistory buildings, consider locating the computer facility on an upper floor to reduce the risk of external penetration and flood damage. Check the roof to insure against water coming through the roof.

6. Separate the computer room, and further separate the tape/disk storage library areas, with noncombustible walls with a minimum fire resistance fire rating of two hours.

7. Do not allow viewing windows into the central computer facility.

8. Provide a separate tape/disk storage vault with fire-resistant walls, a door that will automatically close in case of fire, and proper alarms and automatic fire-retardant dispensing equipment.

9. Seal cement walls and floors with dust-resistant coatings.

10. Be sure that ceilings are watertight so that water cannot leak from floors above.

11. Provide adequate drainage facilities under raised floors because cables with electrical current run under these floors.

12. Be sure that raised flooring has a 12-inch minimum plenum and a 1 in 10 ramp raise.

13. Be sure that there is only one entry and exit door that is used by the personnel of the computer operation center. But all doors should be provided with emergency break-bar openings. These other doors should be alarmed. Equip all doors with adequate locks and nonremovable hinge pins.

14. Install an automatic fire suppression system in the computer facility, and especially within the tape/disk library. The recommended system is a dry contact halogenated agent such as Halon 1301.

15. If overhead water sprinklers are required by the building code, they should be preaction type which are supplied by dry waterpipe charged by the first activation of a fire alarm and released by the fire itself.

16. Install fire and smoke detectors in both ceiling areas of computer facilities and under raised flooring.

17. Install two types of fire and smoke detectors. Ionization detectors can give very early warning of smoke and rate-compensated fire detectors can be used as the automatic triggering mechanism for the fire suppressant.

18. Always have a manual override so should there be a false alarm, authorized personnel can shut down the automatic release of fire-retardant chemicals.

19. Place portable fire extinguishers strategically about the computer center at floor level, but clearly marked from floor to ceiling by a red stripe.

20. Mount floor lifter tools at the areas where portable fire extinguishers are located and duly marked by the floor-to-ceiling red stripe.

21. Insure that the fire-resistant vault (two hours) is large enough to hold very sensitive programs as well as to store data.

22. Be sure that curtains, carpeting, furniture, raised flooring, false ceilings, air-conditioning filters, electrical and acoustical insulating materials, and so on, are made of noncombustible materials or treated with fire-retardant materials.

23. Periodically vacuum under the raised floor to remove paper dust particles.

24. Prohibit smoking and eating of foods and liquids in the computer room and tape vault.

25. Install automatic fire dampeners in the air-conditioning ducts and fresh-air ducts supplying the computer room. This will cut off the flow of air to these areas in case of a fire alarm so it will not feed the flames.

26. Be sure the automatic fire alarm system has the capability to transmit signals to a remote point that is monitored 24 hours per day. This remote point may be a guard station at the organization, or the local fire department.

27. Store paper and other combustible supplies,with the exception of immediate usage requirements, outside the computer room.

28. Provide underwriter laboratories (UL) approved self-extinguishing waste containers.

29. Keep flammable materials used in the computer room, such as cleaning fluids, in small quantities.

30. Insure adequate maintenance of fire and smoke detectors, the fire alarm system, portable fire extinguishers, emergency exits, electrical and power distribution panels, air-conditioning, chilled water, uninterruptible power supplies, diesel generators, and the like.

31. Continually dispose of accumulations of combustible trash.

32. Develop a training program for fire fighting and for the orderly evacuation of the data processing facility in case a fire alarm sounds.

33. If economically justified after the appropriate risk analysis, install an uninterruptible power system (UPS) and/or a backup diesel generator. These systems may offer temporary protection that would allow an orderly shutdown should the normal electrical power fail, or they may offer a long-term electrical backup. These systems should be tested at least monthly.

34. Protect all electrical power serving the central processing unit (CPU), CPU-related equipment, and the data communication equipment from fluctuating electrical loads by utilizing an isolation transformer.

35. Insure that the computer center, especially the CPU, has its own separate incoming power supply and power cables. This may include its own separate transformer and circuits.

36. Protect all computer circuits from malicious vandalism where someone might open the circuits and cut the power. This means providing locking circuit-control boxes and locating circuit-control boxes in locked rooms.

37. Install easily accessible emergency power shutdown controls at all fire exits. Consider two controls, one for both air-conditioning and data processing equipment and one for air-conditioning only.

38. Be sure that the electrical system distribution panel is in a secure area inaccessible to unauthorized persons.

39. Properly mark circuit breaker panels as to the equipment being serviced to permit ready and expeditious reference.

40. Provide battery-powered emergency lights throughout the facility.

41. Ground all electrical equipment and especially the raised floor pedestal grid to enhance personnel safety.

42. Provide separate locked areas for motor generator equipment to insure its safety.

43. Lock the electrical panels and have the electrical panel service motor generator equipment in separate locked areas.

44. Provide a backup motor generator to service the central processing unit generators should the motor running the computer 400-cycle generators become inoperative.

45. Provide proper electrical interface equipment to reduce power surges between the motor generators and the central computer.

46. Provide adequate preventive maintenance for all motor-generator related equipment.

47. Provide a controlled temperature and humidity environment in the computer area. Maintain temperature and humidity charts by means of a continuous recorder.

48. Provide backup air-conditioning capacity, separate from the central building capacity. This implies the capability of running independently of the building air-conditioning system for off-hours data processing, and in emergencies.

49. Be sure that filters and duct linings are of noncombustible materials in the air-conditioning system.

50. Maintain and check the air-conditioning system monthly.

51. Be sure the fresh air supply is filtered before it is drawn into the computer facility.

52. Inspect the air intake ducts at the outside of the building to see if they are at street level where malicious vandalism could cause serious problems.

53. Check these air intake ducts to insure that personnel cannot crawl into the building through them. The personnel might enter the building either from the roof or from the street level through these ducts.

54. Protect the electrical connections and circuit boxes that feed the air-conditioners. Keep these boxes locked and in a separate locked room.

55. Insure adequate tonnage of air-conditioning in case some of it becomes inoperative. Separate floor-mounted air-conditioners offer more reliability because the loss of one or two of these floor-mounted units does not render the central processing unit inoperable.

56. Insure that the controls for the flow of chilled water are kept in separate locked areas to avoid vandalism.

57. Insure that any electrical pumps to pump chilled water are in separate locked areas and that their electrical control panels are in separate locked areas.

58. When chilled water is supplied from an outside or a central source, insure that there is a backup source of chilled water.

59. Trace the flow of the chilled water pipes to insure that they are relatively secure.

60. Trace the flow of electrical circuits throughout the building to insure that they are relatively secure.

61. Adequately insulate chilled water pipes so that they do not drip water (condensation) on computer-related equipment or supplies.

62. Provide an overall master automatic alarm system to give the status of various systems such as fire/smoke detectors, air-conditioning failure, UPS/diesel generator failure, emergency exit usage, intrusion alarms on specific doors or in air-conditioning ducts, water detectors under raised flooring, motion detectors under raised flooring (when perimeter walls do not go to the structural floor), and other alarms and sensors that may go to specialized areas that might be unique to the data processing facility, for instance, motion detectors above the ceiling. These alarm systems should alert computer room personnel, data processing management, and a remote guard post, if one is available in the organization.

63. Provide plastic sheets to cover data processing equipment should water leakage occur from above.

64. When available, keep any portable electrical power generation equipment, water pumping equipment, and other items that might be utilized in a disaster near the computer center.

65. If the facility is in an earthquake area, brace the tops of tape racks and other tall items to prevent tipping and swaying.

66. Enforce the following housekeeping policies:

    — Prohibit eating and drinking in the computer room

    — Clean equipment covers and work surfaces daily

    — Clean floors regularly

— Dump waste baskets and other trash containers outside of the computer room to avoid excess dust

— Unpack equipment and paper supplies outside of the equipment room in order to reduce dust

— Enforce the entry and egress policies for all personnel.

67. Be sure that corridors, aisles, and clearances around data processing equipment are free of obstructions and provide adequate clearance for smooth evacuation flow.

68. Post evacuation route floor plans on the wall at each portable fire extinguisher location.

69. If the computer area is extremely large, consider having air packs available (mandatory if carbon dioxide fire extinguishers are used).

70. Consider utilizing a minicomputer-based badge recording system to restrict access to the central computer area. Use a multilevel access system that requires a higher access level to have entry to the tape library and a lower access level to allow general entry to areas such as computer operations, system development, programming, technical systems programming areas, and the like.

71. Utilize some sort of a man-trap entry system, television recorder to a central guard area, personal identification by shift supervisors, minicomputer badge control system, or other positive entry control procedures to restrict entry of nonauthorized personnel into sensitive areas.

72. Have everyone wear a badge in sensitive areas; visitors should have a different colored badge, and should sign in and be escorted.

73. Do not identify badges as to the organization to which they belong. In that way, a lost badge will be blindly mailed back to a post-office box.

74. Do not allow programmers and systems analysts into the computer room. Do not allow computer operations personnel into the tape library. If these rules must be violated for special reasons, there should be the proper escort and external authorizations.

75. Provide regular maintenance personnel with their own badges, but sign in replacement personnel as if they were visitors.

76. Do not advertise the location of the central computer facility on signs, maps, or the directory listings of the organization.

77. Discourage tours by the public through the computer facility. If a tour is necessary, make sure that two personnel escort the tour. One leading the group and one following.

78. Issue as few access badge control cards as possible.

79. Do not allow packages, briefcases, and handbags into the central computer area, tape library, or other very sensitive areas.

80. When feasible, utilize a 24-hour a day guard service over entry and egress to the computer center.

81. When feasible, utilize a guard type service for the entire building or facility in which the computer center is placed. This is a first level of security and says that only authorized personnel have entered the building. After that, use an interior level of security by restricting access to the computer operations center, and further restricting the access to the tape/disk library.

82. Establish and document security standards, procedures, and guidelines for the computer facility.

83. Establish the position of Computer Security Administrator. This person would be responsible for physical security, data security, standards, and procedures as they relate to the computer facility and all information control.

84. Provide personnel with an education program in security matters, so the responsibility for security is firmly fixed and clearly understood by those having such responsibilities.

85. Develop a monthly or quarterly security education newsletter to continuously monitor and train personnel in security.

86. Develop and implement a plan covering actions to be taken during an on-site temporary emergency such as bomb threat, flooding, a small localized fire, or a temporary disablement of the computer system.

87. Insure that there is adequate physical security from fire, smoke, heat, physical penetration of personnel, and other factors in the area where backup computer tapes and disks are stored. Also review the temperature and relative humidity because tapes and paper products need to be stored within reasonable temperature and relative humidity ranges.

88. Insure that there is an adequate procedure for the movement of backup materials between the central computer site, tape library, and the remote storage site. This would include a written procedure on how the items are to be moved, who will move them, and the cart (locked metal cart) in which they will be moved.

89. Insure that there is an adequate written procedure for the ultimate disposal of various data processing media that are being stored at a remote backup site.

90. Insure that there is an EDP disaster plan to determine who will be decision-maker in charge of the disaster recovery, and the availability and training of sufficiently experienced personnel. This plan should also include:

    — Recovery procedures for reproducing the data processing media.

    — The location of backup media.

    — Who to contact for the backup media.

    — Which files or data bases will be reconstructed first.

    — Where the replacement of computer hardware can be found.

    — Where the replacement of computer software can be found.

    — Help to be expected from vendors.

— Similar computer equipment configurations and their locations.

— Locations of other support equipment, such as motor generators, air-conditioning, and the like.

— The location of alternative data communication facilities.

— Action to be taken in case of partial unexpected damage.

— Procedures for imposing extraordinary controls during the disaster and until the system returns to normal.

— The location of the disaster plan, which should be stored off-site.

91. Determine whether a paper shredder is necessary to destroy sensitive computer listings, carbon paper, and other security items. A paper shredder may not be adequate and the facility may have to go to a special disposal company or repulp the computer printouts.

92. Insure that there are adequate tape/disk management systems so only the proper tape/disks are scratched and they are not held for an inordinate time.

93. Insure that management is enforcing the policies and procedures with regard to physical security.

94. Insure that management is lending its assistance to the education and training efforts with regard to physical security.

95. Insure that management has considered security as a line item in its budget.

96. Depending on the sensitivity of the system, protect against "eavesdropping" or "phone taps" through electrical emanations from the data processing equipment.

97. Secure all windows, because not only can something be thrown in but something can also be thrown out of the computer facility, such as a disk.

98. Magnets are usually not a problem because they must almost touch a tape or disk to destroy the data. If these are considered to be a problem then install devices around doorways to detect if someone is bringing either magnetized material or steel (such as a gun) into the computer room.

99. Avoid radar within line of sight of a computer. It may interfere with the proper operation of the computer itself. Electromagnetic radiations (microwave ovens) may also interfere with the correct operation of a computer.

100. Have the personnel review the printouts from the minicomputer access system to determine who entered the areas and when they entered them.

101. Determine whether employees in the computer center should sign a statement acknowledging the fact that they should not sell computer programs, use the computer for their own personal or monetary gain, and other such items.

102. Review the data processing media insurance; special policies can be written to cover risks of loss or damage to active data processing media, programs, or instruction media, and all data or information stored upon this media.

103. Review the insurance covering data processing hardware; it is desirable that the hardware policy cover losses on a new replacement cost basis. Usually the blanket building insurance does not cover the value of the data processing equipment, although it may cover special data processing building costs, including raised flooring, special lighting, special electrical circuits, and air-conditioning equipment. When calculating equipment replacement costs, such items as freight charges, testing and debugging expenses, spare parts, and any materials and supplies required should be included. It may be necessary to include specific coverage for equipment at locations other than the primary data processing center. The person responsible for leased equipment should be identified.

104. Review the business interruption and extra expense insurance; if the data processing equipment or media are destroyed there might be a substantial loss of net profit from current operations. Because the organization depends upon instantaneous availability of the computer system, business interruption insurance should be investigated. Insurance is available in various forms to cover loss of income resulting from damage to described property by an insured peril, including the extra expenses of continuing normal operations to the extent that such extra expenses reduce the loss that would have otherwise been incurred. Extra expense insurance pays any extra expenses incurred in using alternative facilities to continue normal computer or data processing operations. This insurance comes into force if there is a provable loss of income because of the interruption in data processing operations. Extra expense insurance can be purchased under a data processing policy covering loss from destruction of or damage to EDP equipment or media and damage to the premises or to the air-conditioning/electrical systems. Such insurance generally provides a stated limit of liability without monthly limitation and insures for a period judged adequate for the repair or replacement of the property lost or damaged.

105. Review the errors and omissions insurance; data processing services sold to outside customers usually expose the organization to a potential liability for financial loss resulting from error, omission, negligence, malicious acts, dishonesty of employees, or faulty results due to machine malfunctions. It may be desirable to have insurance against potential liabilities.

106. Review the valuable papers and records insurance policies; data processing media represent one form of valuable documents and records; valuable papers represent a second. Valuable papers and records insurance may be added to most special data processing policies or may be expanded to include data processing media. It is best to provide that the recovery will be the actual cost of reproduction or replacement of the valuable paper or records.

107. Determine whether there is a periodic evaluation of the necessary insurance for the entire data processing facility.

108. On leased equipment, determine whether the vendor has adequate insurance or if the organization would be responsible for some perils that may be excluded from the vendor's insurance.

DATA BASE CONTROL MATRIX

This chapter defines and discusses the control review matrix that might be used when reviewing data base controls. The controls/safeguards listed in this matrix are specifically designed for reviewing data-base-oriented data repositories with regard to integrity and control.

THE MATRIX APPROACH

The internal control area to be reviewed using this matrix covers data base controls. These data base controls involve the controls surrounding a data base or data management system and pertain directly to the data base and to the administrative functions associated with data-base-oriented systems. When reviewing the data base controls, match each resource/asset with its corresponding concern/exposure as listed in Figure 9-1: Data Base Control Matrix. This matrix lists the resources in relation to the potential exposures and cross-relates these with the various controls/safeguards that should be considered when reviewing data base integrity and control (see chapter 1 for an explanation on how to use the control matrix approach).

Immediately following the matrix is a definition of each of the concerns/exposures that are listed across the top of the matrix and each of the resources/assets that are listed down the left vertical column of the matrix. Following these definitions is a complete numerical listing and description of each of the controls/safeguards that are listed numerically in the cells of the matrix.

CONCERNS/EXPOSURES

The following concerns/exposures are those that are directly applicable to the data base functions for on-line and batch systems. The definition for each of these exposures, listed across the top of the matrix, is as follows:

- Access Control—Control of the access of individuals into and out of the data base itself. This concern involves allowing some users to have access to certain areas and others to have access to all areas of the data base (this specifically involves controlling the data base administrator and other systems programming type of personnel).

- Information Control Policies—The degree of control implemented by the management of the organization. This concern includes the handling of information within the organization and especially that information directly related to the data base. It is specifically related to the control of information flow, the uses to which information may be put, and to who can have access to what information as well as to *how information should be disposed of or destroyed* after its useful need has passed.

CONCERNS / EXPOSURES

RESOURCES / ASSETS

	ACCESS CONTROL	INFORMATION CONTROL POLICIES	FRAUD AND DEFALCATION	PRIVACY	DISASTER AND DISRUPTION	TRANSACTION ERROR HANDLING	AUDIT TRAILS	OUTPUT BALANCING AND RECONCILIATION	PROGRAM INTERFACES	
DATA BASE ADMINISTRATOR	2,5,9,12,15,17 19,21-24,32,33 39, 48, 51-53, 63, 64	1-18, 20, 22, 24-26, 28, 29, 32, 35, 36, 38, 39,42-44,48,49 51, 52, 59	2,4,5,9,11, 13-16,18,19, 21-24,32,33,41, 47, 50	2, 4, 5, 9, 11, 13-16, 18, 19, 21-24, 32, 33, 41, 47, 50	1, 6-8, 13, 16, 42, 47, 57, 63	2, 5, 6, 8, 13, 16	2, 16, 25, 41, 50	2, 16	3, 13, 32	
DATA BASE SOFTWARE	3, 4, 36, 45, 53	36	32, 33, 34	32, 33, 34	36		53			
			SEE CHAPTER 10 FOR MOST OF THESE CONTROLS							
LOGGING AND REPORTING	45	2, 16, 28, 35	16, 20, 21, 26, 28, 35	16, 20, 21, 26, 28, 35	16, 26, 28	28	16, 26, 28, 40, 48	28		
DATA BASE OPERATIONAL STANDARDS	8, 45, 54, 55	1, 6-10, 22, 23, 28-30, 54-56, 58	8, 22, 23, 54	8, 22, 23, 54	6-8, 13, 16, 30 57, 58	16, 30, 56-59	40	29	22, 54-57 59	
DATA DICTIONARY	22, 40, 43, 45	14, 32, 33, 35, 37, 38, 40-44	22, 40, 41, 43, 44	22, 40, 41, 43, 44		45	37, 40, 41	38, 40, 45		
PHYSICAL AND DATA SECURITY	5, 12, 24-26, 28, 31, 46, 52 53, 64	4,5,8,12,15,16, 18-24, 30, 31, 46, 51, 52, 58, 63, 64	4, 5,12, 19-27, 31, 43, 47, 49 51-53, 63, 64	4, 5, 12, 19-27, 31, 43, 47, 49, 51-53, 63, 64	7, 8, 19, 26, 30 47, 63	26, 46	16, 20, 25, 26, 46	46	34, 46	
PEOPLE	9, 23, 28, 31, 48, 50, 52, 54	1, 8, 9, 23, 27, 31, 44, 48-50, 60-62	2, 3, 5, 9, 16, 18, 23-27, 31, 48-50, 52, 54	2, 3, 5, 9, 16, 18, 23-27, 31, 48-50, 52, 54	57, 63	5, 56, 58-60	25-27, 50, 56	29	54, 62	

FIGURE 9-1: DATA BASE CONTROL MATRIX

- Fraud and Defalcation—The safeguarding of the data base's assets from unauthorized use or removal by persons trusted by the organization (employees, vendors, etc.) or outsiders who are not directly related with the organization. This exposure involves embezzlement or some other type of act where the individual involved ends up with a personal gain.

- Privacy—The accidental or intentional release of data about an individual, assuming that the release of this personal information was improper to the normal conduct of the business at the organization.

- Disaster and Disruption—The major interruption of the continued use of the data base. This concern would include both the intentional or unintentional destruction or partial destruction (fire, flood, etc.) of the data base so it could not operate in its normal fashion.

- Transaction Error Handling—The methodologies and controls for handling errors after they have been entered into the data base, correcting these errors, and reentering the corrected data into the data base. This concern involves both the updating and downdating of data bases as well as the temporary backup of data bases; it also involves the restarting of data base management programs that have failed during their normal course of processing.

- Audit Trails—Insurance that the data can be traced backward and forward through the entire data base update or downdate functions.

- Output Balancing and Reconciliation—The responsibility for monitoring the data base-related controls and insuring that data has not been lost during the updating or downdating of the data base itself.

- Program Interfaces—The interface between the data base management programs, other software within the computer (operating system, telecommunications access methods, teleprocessing monitors, etc.), and the application programs themselves.

RESOURCES/ASSETS

The following resources/assets are those that should be reviewed during the data base control review. The definition for each of these assets, listed down the left vertical column of the matrix, is as follows:

- Data Base Administrator—The person who is responsible for maintaining and controlling the data base. This person is responsible for the data dictionary, the data base access method software, the overall data structures, and any other related facets of the data base.

- Data Base Software—The specific programs that are utilized to access the data, update data bases, and interface with any other programs (operating systems and applications programs) that are utilized in the overall data processing system and that relate to the data base itself.

- Logging and Reporting—The historical record of any data base. This resource is to be construed as any and all output reports that can be used to control or to trace back what was entered into or removed from the data base. This also includes those output reports that show any type of "systems" changes that were made to the data base, the data base dictionary, the software, and the like.

- Data Base Operational Standards—The written documentation of the structure of the data base, the operational characteristics of the data base, the data dictionary, and any other written documentation that relates to the data base in any fashion.

- Data Dictionary—The list of the data elements within the data base. This resource is listed because it is vital that the data base administrator have an orderly listing of all data definitions.

- Physical and Data Security—Any special aspect of physical security over the data base or data security that protects the data base. This resource would involve special security type programs or protective software that might be involved as well as other restrictions, and might be interrelated with the overall physical security of the data processing operations, including where the data bases are physically housed.

- People—The users of the data base, the individuals responsible for the data processing operations, programming, systems development, and for any other operations that are performed during the development of or daily operation of the data bases.

CONTROLS/SAFEGUARDS

The following controls/safeguards should be considered when reviewing the data base functions for on-line and batch systems. This numerical listing describes each control.

It should be noted that implementation of various controls can be both costly and time consuming. It is of great importance that a realistic and pragmatic evaluation be made with regard to the probability of a specific exposure affecting a specific asset. Only then can the control for safeguarding the asset be evaluated in a cost-effective manner.

The controls, as numerically listed in the cells of the matrix, are as follows: *

1. Insure that the data base administrator (DBA) is responsible for the overall education of users and technical staff in the concepts and workings of the data base (see control 39).

2. Insure that the DBA monitors the usage of the data base; in other words, the DBA should monitor the record-keeping and other statistics functions such as who has access to the data base, which programs can access the data base, response statistics, and any other statistics that can be used to control the data base.

3. Insure that only the DBA has the authority to make changes to the data base management system (DBMS) library. These changes should be performed by the DBA because the DBA is independent of both application programming development and the users.

---

* DBA—Data Base Administrator (a person)

DBMS—Data Base Management System (software)

4. Do not allow the DBA to have unsupervised access to the computer operations area and do not allow the DBA to operate the computers.

5. Insure that the DBA is not able to initiate transactions without user departmental approval; the DBA should have external authorization before entering transaction data.

6. Have the DBA establish written procedures for the recovery of the data base in the event of total or partial destruction.

7. Insure that the DBA is responsible for the integrity of the data base and develops the validation rules and other decisions that affect data quality as well as protection against destruction.

8. Have the DBA establish written procedures for security of the data base (protection of the data base against accidental or deliberate destruction and/or unauthorized access). This would also include concurrence and deadlock type of conflicting requirements.

9. Insure that the DBA consults with users with regard to data organization and methods of retrieval and extraction. The application programmer should only know the program specification information required for the program to operate and for access to the needed data elements. The application programmer does not need to know data in the data base not directly associated with the specific application for which he or she is responsible.

10. Have the DBA document the contents of the data base, define the entities and attributes, and define all entity interrelationships.

11. Insure that the DBA has control of the contents, organization, integrity, and privacy of the data base (logical).

12. Insure that the DBA is consulted about and has control of the data base storage environment (physical).

13. Insure that the DBA is consulted about and has control of the operating environment of the data base such as user interface, monitoring, scheduling, and recovery.

14. Insure that the DBA has control of and is responsible for the development and maintenance of the data dictionary.

15. Insure that the DBA is responsible for the overall security requirements of the data base management system in its entirety.

16. Insure that the DBA is responsible for the development of and monitoring of various statistics and other reports such as reviewing the console log and other output devices or media with regard to initial access to permanent records, modifications to the data base, execution of data base programs, modification of system records, save/reconstruction/restart type procedures, authorization tables, security matrices, and other statistics provided by the data base management system, as well as any special DBA or vendor utilities.

17. Insure that the DBA function is independent of data processing and user management.

18. Insure that the DBA provides the auditors and/or system designers with

the primary input with regard to any matters concerning the security and control of all data base files.

19. Insure that the live data base is separate from the data base used for program testing (there should be a test data base).

20. Determine whether the vendor-supplied specially written utility programs are under the control of the data base administrator. Whenever these utilities are utilized, a log should be kept of who used the utility and when. Utilities for initial loading of data bases, compression of items, and items deleted from data bases should be specially controlled.

21. Periodically review the computer system operations log (console) and any special DBMS logs in order to monitor access and other control features involved with the data base and DBMS software.

22. Provide special procedures to prevent access to the data base when the data base is not under the control of the DBMS software. This is especially important because the physical data base would still exist, and might be subjected to an unauthorized copy attempt.

23. Adequately control access to the data base, DBMS library, and any other documentation by utility programs, application programs, users, or any other means. Utility programs for listing the data base descriptions, testing the data, or any other type of listing should be specially controlled and continually monitored.

24. Review access through an on-line data communication oriented network (see chapter 4: Data Communication Control Matrix) in order to insure that there are adequate controls with regard to the data communication network that is being utilized.

25. Especially review any input/output access devices located within the computer operations area to insure that they are adequately controlled as far as physical access and that there is some method of tracing back to see who made which entries through that specific input/output device.

26. Review the specific software controls that are utilized to limit access to data bases. Examples of these types of controls are:

    — Tag input requests to identify the terminal, time, and operator from which the input came.

    — Lock out users from parts of the data base that are not needed for the performance of their job.

    — Severely limit changes and updating of data base files with regard to different users.

    — Log all transactions for control, audit, and recovery.

    — Severely control the access when purging the contents of a data base.

    — Severely control the access when reorganizing a data base or compressing data.

    — Limit the number of personnel that can request and have access to test data bases.

27. Insure that all changes and system utility commands are entered from one "master" terminal. Physical access and logical access to this terminal should be severely restricted.

28. Review the data base logging function to determine whether the data base log records the following:

    — All new data introduced into the data base such as the before and after image of each data base update.

    — All data deleted from a data base.

    — The origin of all transactions, internal or external.

    — Data base utilization by application.

    — Data base utilization by individual users.

    — Security violations with regard to the data base.

    — Reorganizations/compressions of the data base.

    — The use of data base systems utilities.

    — Record of systems status that may be required for restart or backouts of erroneous data.

    — Records of various accounting information.

29. Insure that there are procedure manuals and operating instructions for all application programs that access the data base (only the portions accessing or controlling the data base need be discussed at this point of the review).

30. Provide a written procedure delineating the provision for backup and recovery procedures should the data base fail, be partially destroyed, or be totally destroyed.

31. Insure that only computer operations personnel have access to the computer operations area where the data base files are stored.

32. Be sure the DBA approves and logs all changes to the DBMS library. This control is needed to insure that only required data items are accessed by an application program.

33. Be sure the DBA periodically reviews the DBMS library to insure that no unauthorized changes have been made.

34. Provide a special software program that periodically looks over the physical data base and looks for unexplained (holes) in the physical data structure or the logical structure.

35. Provide a log of programs run. The program specification used by the program should be maintained and periodically reviewed by the DBA. This control provides additional insurance that only authorized program specification information was used to access the data in the data base. This may also reveal temporary changes made to the DBMS library.

36. Have the DBA approve all major modifications (both in-house and vendor

supplied) to the DBMS software. He or she should not blindly accept vendor modifications to their software package without testing and making a management decision as to whether to incorporate a new version.

37. Provide a data dictionary for simple effective control over all data definitions and to trace the path of data through the system itself. Establishment of a data dictionary is the initial step in the design and implementation of any data base system.

38. Insure that the DBA is responsible for the development and continuous monitoring of the data dictionary.

39. Provide a human function entitled Data Base Administrator. This is the key individual responsible for the overall data base.

40. Insure that the proper audit trails or management trails are included in the data dictionary. The data dictionary is the audit trail of the data base because it supplies program/data relationships and can provide the tool to trace valid but incorrect data, edit, validate, and make available various other information required for security and control of a data base.

41. Insure that all changes to the data base (permanent data changes) are entered into the data dictionary and are approved by the DBA. These changes should emanate from the user, the programmer, or the analyst involved in the application program development. Any permanent changes requested by the DBA should be approved by some other authority such as the user, the manager of data processing, the organization's computer security administrator, or the like.

42. Restrict the distribution of the data dictionary and store copies of the data dictionary in a safe storage area (only the DBA should have copies of the data dictionary).

43. Allow auditors and system designers to review the data dictionary when necessary but only under the auspices of the DBA.

44. Have an EDP auditor specifically review the security descriptions in the data dictionary, identify the data elements that are particularly sensitive, and concentrate the review and effort on those elements and the specific control thereof.

45. Provide specific edit tests. The data dictionary should contain all the details that govern and describe these edit tests. These edit tests are usually performed on data before a data base master record is updated or downdated.

46. Whenever possible, utilize generalized audit software to review specific data base files even though most audit software available today does not access the files in the same manner in which the data base accesses the files. In other words, most audit software will flatten the files and read them onto a tape in a serial fashion.

47. Consider developing different scenarios that might involve deliberate attempts to destroy or defraud a data base (consider both internal and external threats). These scenarios should be developed by the DBA. The penetrations depicted by the scenarios might be carried out by authorized or unauthorized personnel changing the data dictionary, modifying the application programs (program specification block), using system or vendor utilities to access the data base, physically stealing copies of the data base or data dictionary,

randomly scanning the data base files to look for restricted data, improperly using "legal" passwords, obtaining access to hard-copy output (used carbon paper), wiretapping the data communication network (although this is very remote), and performing any other illegal penetration or manipulation.

48. Review the user controls with regard to security. These controls would keep unauthorized users out of the system and also control how authorized users could use the system. These controls may include a simple user password, written or other procedural controls within a department, separation of duties, system logs, and the like. User controls are also contained in the matrices in chapters 2 on General Organizational Control and 3 on Input Control of this book.

49. Review the on-line terminal/distributed systems controls with regard to security. These controls are covered in chapter 7 of this book.

50. Review the "job control" with regard to security of batch-oriented data bases. Each production job can only access a certain file or set of files in a data base and it can use those files for specific functions. Also, each specific transaction (on-line system) should only be able to access a certain file or set of files in a data base. Review, with the DBA, whether one production job or transaction can access another production job or transaction which in turn would allow access to data for which the original production job or transaction was not authorized.

51. Review the data base file controls with regard to security. In other words, are there any levels of security such as top secret, secret, confidential, company confidential, private, or the like?

52. When reviewing the data base, also review some general types of security (physical security is covered in chapter 8 of this book). Examples are as follows:

    — Insure adequate physical security of the physical data base.

    — Use passwords, lockwords, or personal identification.

    — Provide for employee security training (one-time course work) and the continuous reeducation through further courses and a periodic security newsletter.

    — Insure continual monitoring of employees in sensitive positions, such as the DBA.

    — Identify the risks of improper access and destruction of the data base.

    — Review both the automated and manual administrative controls for access control and modifications (some of these may be in chapter 5 of this book: Program/Computer Processing Control Matrix).

53. Consider an extreme form of control, for instance, a directory of access privileges at the file or record level correlated with a security profile of each user, user department, or terminal station.

54. Insure that there are proper documentation and programming standards for application programs. There should be written standards for application programs to specify the data language calls that can be used to access the data base.

55. Insure that there are written documentation standards for all application programs. The documentation should be reviewed by the DBA before the program is put into production. Documentation is more critical in data base systems because a common data base is accessed by multiple programs, whereas in file-oriented systems, a specific file is mounted for a specific program.

56. Insure that there are program testing standards that specify criteria for generating test data base data, reviewing the test results, and retaining the test data base end results. These controls are more important in a data base environment because of the cascading effect of errors that may be caused by an application program error.

57. Insure that backup and recovery procedures are tested in the application programs prior to implementation. These recovery and restart procedures should delineate the recovery of data bases or parts thereof and the recovery of transactions as well as the restart of application programs and systems software such as the DBMS, the transaction controller software, the operating system software, and the like. This involves backup and recovery of the data base and its interrelationship with specific application programs.

58. Insure that there is specific documentation for the backup and recovery of an entire data base. This could involve copying over the data base at frequent intervals (only viable when the data base is small) or the appropriate logging functions to either update or downdate a data base. This would involve the procedures for automatic recovery, the standards and procedures for partial recovery or restart, and the verification of data integrity with regard to the last transaction processed, a double update, or a lost transaction.

59. Review the testing program. In order to carry out an adequate testing program, there should be several different types of data bases such as:

    — The unit test data base used by the design team to debug the original program.

    — The internal audit test data base used to test systems prior to conversion and prior to pilot operations.

    — Benchmark test data bases used to test program revisions during pilot or production changes or post-implementation audits.

    — Production data bases used to process daily activity.

60. Review the user interface and opinions by interviewing the users to determine whether they feel that the application programs/data bases have been adequately tested and whether they were involved in the final stages of testing. An experienced user can usually provide valuable information on program and data base testing.

61. See that whenever possible, the EDP auditor participates in data base development, data base changes, and application program development and changes during the new system development life cycle or the system enhancement cycle.

62. Data bases interact with many other areas. See that the EDP auditor keeps in mind that the data base audit does not encompass all the various functional responsibilities that are inherent in a major on-line data base-oriented system. Some of these responsibilities with regard to the data base are data base

administration, data communication administration, application system development, application programming, system programming, data processing operations, remote branch (terminal) operations, and master terminal control operations (could include both data processing and data communications).

63. Review the overall physical security (see chapter 8 of this book) with regard to the data base.

64. Insure that the authorization tables that authorize user passwords or restrict other users in any way are safe and secure. Review both their physical safety and their logical security. Typical authorization tables referred to here might be as follows:

— Transaction type: A specific user might be restricted from certain types of transactions.

— Programs: Users might be restricted to certain processing programs.

— Group files: Users might be permitted to access, modify, and delete only specific data from specific files.

— Complete files: Access might be given to a complete set of files.

— Individual records: Access might be restricted to specific records.

— Groups of records: Specific users might be permitted or restricted to use only specific groups of records.

— Group items: Segments in a data base or combinations of these might be restricted to certain users.

— Various password controls: Users might be restricted to certain portions of the data base.

— Various terminal controls: Various terminals might be transaction coded so as to restrict them to certain portions of the data base.

— Circuit controls: Certain circuits in a data communication network might be restricted to certain portions of the data base.

— Lockwords: The lockwords or authorization bits for data base protection might be cross-related to a user, terminal, or other logical or physical item. They could relate to items such as job number, individual user, groups of users, security level, application programs, terminals, and the like.

SYSTEM SOFTWARE CONTROL MATRIX

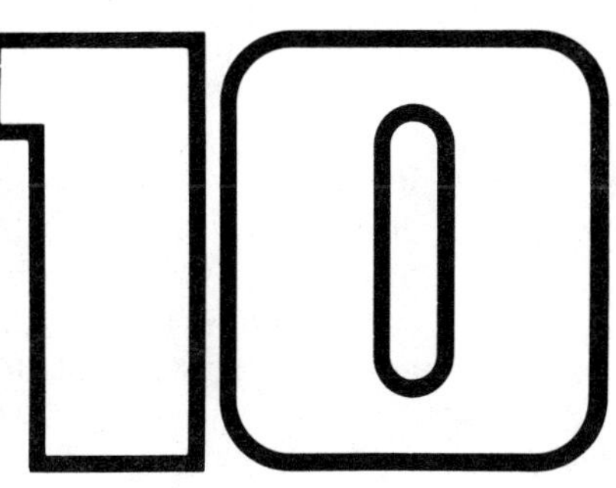

This chapter defines and discusses the control review matrix that might be used when reviewing system software controls. The controls/safeguards listed in this matrix are specifically designed for reviewing system software such as operating systems, data communication software, data base management systems software, and the like. Application program controls are listed in chapter 5: Program/Computer Processing Control Matrix.

THE MATRIX APPROACH

The internal control area to be reviewed using this matrix covers system software controls. These system software controls may involve operating system software, data communication software, data base management system software, and other sophisticated programs that enable the computer to operate. When reviewing the system software controls, match each resource/asset with its corresponding concern/exposure as listed in Figure 10-1: System Software Control Matrix. This matrix lists the resources in relation to the potential exposures and cross-relates these with the various controls/safeguards that should be considered when reviewing system software controls (see chapter 1 for an explanation on how to use the control matrix approach).

Immediately following the matrix is a definition of each of the concerns/exposures that are listed across the top of the matrix and each of the resources/assets that are listed down the left vertical column of the matrix. Following these definitions is a complete numerical listing and description of each of the controls/safeguards that are listed numerically in the cells of the matrix.

CONCERNS/EXPOSURES

The following concerns/exposures are those that are directly applicable to the review of the system software for computer-based systems. The definition for each of these exposures, listed across the top of the matrix, is as follows:

- Errors and Omissions—The accidental or intentional creation of an error during the processing or running of any aspect of the computer system software. This also includes the accidental or intentional omission of data (loss) during the running of any of the software programs.

- Unauthorized Program Changes—The temporary or permanent change of program code by individuals who are unauthorized to make these changes, as well as by individuals who are so authorized but who make illegal program changes for whatever reason.

- Security/Theft—The security or theft of information or software programs that should have been kept confidential because of their proprietary nature. In a way, this is a form of privacy, but the information removed from the organization does not pertain to an individual. The information or software programs might be inadvertently (accidentally) removed from the organization, or might be the subject of an outright theft.

- Program/Data Validation—The software program editing of data, job control, or some specific preprogrammed actions that may be taken. This involves default options, should the operations personnel not properly specify a specific option, and may also include the discovery of omissions in certain parts of the software.

- Restart and Recovery—The restarting of software programs that have failed during their normal course of processing and the recovery that should take place so no data is lost, erroneously processed, or processed twice because of the failure (the failure may have been caused by a software failure, an application program failure, or a computer hardware failure).

- Audit Trails/Documentation—Insuring that the flow of information throughout the software can be traced backward and forward through the entire processing cycle. This exposure is also concerned with the adequate documentation of the software.

- Error Handling—The procedures and methods used to insure that all errors, rejected data, and other perturbations are properly recorded and accounted for during the running of the software. This involves accounting for and detecting errors, loss, and reporting these errors.

- Program Access Control—Control of the access of individuals to the software. This concern is specifically aimed at insuring that only proper and authorized personnel utilize the system software, the special utilities, and that there are *no illegal penetrations* into any of the system software.

- Programmed Controls—Any internally programmed checking routines or other reporting routines that are built into the software. These internal programmed routines, within the software package, should prevent and detect any erroneous or illegal actions, and should also report upon any suspicious actions.

RESOURCES/ASSETS

The following resources/assets are those that should be reviewed during the system software control review. The definition for each of these assets, listed down the left vertical column of the matrix, is as follows:

- Operating System Software—The overall software that runs the entire computerized system. This resource includes the operating system supplied by the computer vendor and specifically includes the system supervisory programs, bootstrap programs, and any other type of software programs utilized to run the overall computer system.

- Data Communication Software—The software programs that are utilized to run the data communication portions of the system. The programs are specifically concerned with the telecommunications access methods, the telecommunications monitors that may oversee the entire data communication function, and any front-end communication processor software. Front-end software might be remotely located with regard to the central communication

CONCERNS / EXPOSURES

RESOURCES / ASSETS	ERRORS AND OMISSIONS	UNAUTHORIZED PROGRAM CHANGES	SECURITY/ THEFT	PROGRAM/ DATA VALIDATION	RESTART AND RECOVERY	AUDIT TRAILS/ DOCUMENTATION	ERROR HANDLING	PROGRAM ACCESS CONTROL	PROGRAMMED CONTROLS	
OPERATING SYSTEM SOFTWARE	3,10-14,16,19, 20, 37, 41, 42, 45, 55, 59	1-5, 10-14, 16, 19, 20, 24, 36, 42, 44-50	10-14, 16, 19, 20, 24, 32, 36, 38-40, 42, 44-50, 52-55 61, 62	2,7,8,9,13, 24, 67	5, 6, 10, 14, 23 26, 32, 33, 35, 60	10-14, 16, 19, 20, 24, 29. 42, 44, 58	9, 13, 21, 58, 66-68	3, 10-14, 16,19, 20, 22, 24, 32-34, 36, 42, 44-51, 53, 54 57-60	7, 8, 10, 11, 17-19, 23, 24, 34, 41, 42, 54, 56-59, 65, 67, 68	
DATA COMMUNICATION SOFTWARE	10, 11, 19, 37, 55, 59	1-5, 10, 11, 19, 24, 36, 49	10, 11, 19, 24, 36, 52-55, 61,62	2, 7, 8, 9, 13, 32, 67	5, 6, 23, 26, 32-35, 60	19, 24, 58	9, 13, 58, 66-68	16, 19, 22, 24, 33, 34, 36, 49, 51, 53, 54, 57-59	7, 8, 10, 18, 23, 24, 34, 54, 56-58, 65, 67, 68	
DISTRIBUTED INTELLIGENCE SOFTWARE	3, 10, 11, 19, 37, 55, 59	1-5, 10, 11, 19, 24, 36	10, 11, 19, 24, 36, 38-40 52-55, 61, 62	2, 7, 8, 9 ,13, 32, 67	5, 6, 23, 26, 32-35, 60	19, 24, 58	9, 13, 58, 66-68	3, 16, 19, 22, 24, 33, 34, 36, 51, 53, 54, 57-59.	7, 8, 10, 18, 23, 24, 34, 54, 56-58, 65, 67, 68	
DATA BASE MANAGEMENT SYSTEMS SOFTWARE	21, 37, 55, 59	1-5, 21, 24, 28, 36, 46	21, 24, 36, 38-40, 52, 53, 55, 61, 62	7, 8, 9, 32, 67	5, 6, 23, 26, 32, 35, 60	4, 21, 24, 58	9, 66, 67	4, 16, 21,22,24, 28, 33, 36, 46, 51, 53, 57, 59	7, 8, 10, 18, 23, 24, 28, 56-58, 65, 67, 68	
ADMINISTRATIVE POLICIES	1, 5, 6, 10-15, 19-21, 39	4, 5, 7, 10-15, 19-21, 25-29, 39, 43, 44, 61, 63, 67	7, 10-15, 19-21, 27-31, 39, 40, 42-44, 52, 61, 63, 67		5, 6, 13, 26, 30,35	1, 5-7, 10-15, 19-21, 27, 29, 30, 42-44, 61-63, 67	6	5, 7, 10-15, 19-22, 25-31, 39, 40, 42, 51, 52, 61-63		
DOCUMENTATION	8-11, 16-20	2, 4, 7, 9, 10, 11, 16-20	7, 9, 10, 11, 16-20, 25		8	2, 4, 7, 9, 10, 11, 16-20	8	2, 4, 7, 9, 10, 11, 16-20, 25, 67		
SYSTEMS SOFTWARE PERSONNEL	9	9, 26, 38, 63-67	9, 38-40, 64 66, 67	63-66	30, 35	9, 63-65, 67	9	9, 26, 29, 30, 38, 64, 66, 67		

FIGURE 10-1: SYSTEM SOFTWARE CONTROL MATRIX

center. This software review may also involve data communication software located at remote concentrator sites or the data communication software located at remote intelligent terminal devices.

- Distributed Intelligence Software—The operational software (not application programs) that is located at distributed data processing sites. This resource is specifically aimed at software packages that are distributed at the remote ends of the data communication links, but these packages do not include the data communication aspects; they only include the distributed intelligence for running distributed data processing sites.

- Data Base Management Systems Software (DBMS)—The data base management software that resides in the central computer, a back-end computer, or at a remote distributed site (assumes distributed data bases) and specifically controls the accesses to and from the data base.

- Administrative Policies—The policies, procedures, and records that are concerned with the development of, control of, and storage of any of the software packages.

- Documentation—The review of the documentation of any of the system software packages.

- Systems Software Personnel—The specific controls that should be in place to insure that the systems programmers and other highly technical personnel perform their duties in both an efficient and accurate manner, as well as insuring that they do not perform any extraneous duties that might be harmful to the organization.

CONTROLS/SAFEGUARDS

The following controls/safeguards should be considered when reviewing the system software for computer-based systems. This numerical listing describes each control.

It should be noted that implementation of various controls can be both costly and time consuming. It is of great importance that a realistic and pragmatic evaluation be made with regard to the probability of a specific exposure affecting a specific asset. Only then can the control for safeguarding the asset be evaluated in a cost-effective manner.

The controls, as numerically listed in the cells of the matrix, are as follows:

1. Maintain a check-sum count of the "bits" in the software packages. In this way, a quick check can be made to see if there are the same number of bits; the organization can then rest assured that there probably have not been any modifications to the software program.

2. When feasible, conduct either source code comparisons or object code comparisons (some organizations have conducted source-to-object code comparisons) in order to determine that there have not been any changes since the last source or object code comparison. This control is very time consuming and involves the validation of a specific program on a line-by-line basis and comparing that same program at some future time to the validated version.

3. When sensitive software is utilized at distributed sites, consider downline loading that software from the central site. This would provide the assurance that no illegal program changes have been made at the remote site. Also,

new programs could be downline loaded every time a vendor conducted maintenance.

4. Utilize generalized audit software to review various functions of the systems software packages and distribute these generalized audit software packages to personnel at remote sites. At the central site the auditors or system designers would conduct this function.

5. Regularly review the logs of system restarts and accountings of rerun time due to system malfunctions.

6. Insure that there is a trouble log regarding software and that it contains the diagnosis of each problem and that the person, software component, or device that caused the malfunction can be isolated. Consider developing statistical reports from these logs and initiate appropriate actions if patterns emerge.

7. Insure that all security features that were built into any of the system software packages have been considered and if they are not being used, determine the reason or reasons why.

8. Determine whether there are cleanly programmed and well-defined interfaces between any system software packages such as between operating systems, data communication software, distributed intelligence software, data base management systems, and the like.

9. Determine whether the system software programmers have enumerated all the known loopholes in any of the software and that they have ascertained the degree of exposure attributable to each loophole and made possible corrections.

10. If the system is running any type of a queuing system, such as paging or data communication input/output transactions, review the queues, space management, and other dynamic allocation spaces in order to insure that a user cannot get out of its address space and violate another user space or the operating system.

11. Insure that there are no "back door" entrances to any of the system software that would allow the security protections to be violated or confused (sometimes called hooks to which a user can attach its own special routines). Determine whether it is possible to chain these open accesses in such a way that the operating system becomes disoriented and gives an application program supervisor state. In other words, can the operating system be read or overlaid by adroitly manipulated input/output extents even though the commands that initiate input/output may be controlled in the supervisor mode?

12. Determine whether each usage of the load button on the computer console is recorded and insure that someone checks that every program load is required and that all previous files are off-line whenever the secure operating system is not in control of the computer.

13. Review the safeguards with regard to the console operator illegally resetting the internal computer time of day clock, and insure that either this cannot be done or that there are adequate secondary controls so it will be clearly known when and by whom this was done.

14. Insure that there are always two operators present whenever changes of

the values in memory are entered from the master console for whatever reason.

15. Whenever there is a second or alternate master operator's console, insure that it too is under constant surveillance and that all of its console actions are written on the audit log just as they would be from the master console.

16. Determine whether the system software is programmed to dynamically test bounds registers and other security hardware features before giving control to an application program.

17. Determine whether a violation of a security protection causes a job or transaction to be instantly aborted and a message to be written on the master security terminal or wherever.

18. Determine whether various segments of the system software are protected either by passwords (individual user's security codes) or lockwords (software security codes) or by hardware-protection for various areas of memory.

19. Insure that repeated log-on failures are recorded and that some sort of positive action is taken such as shutting down the offending terminal and contacting the appropriate security personnel.

20. Insure that system software commands can only be entered from one master terminal and not from a set of terminals. Also insure that it is impossible to configure a remote terminal as a master command terminal.

21. Insure that the data base management system protects against concurrence and deadlock and that all file accesses are logged on some sort of an audit log.

22. Insure that any special utility programs that would be used with any of the system software packages are adequately controlled and not at the disposal of general programmers or computer operators.

23. Insure that the operating system and other software packages take snapshots of the status of the computer for restart purposes, and that the proper logging has taken place for restart purposes.

24. Consider having the system software check-sum its own sensitive internal tables and revalidate these check-sums periodically in order to guard against a sophisticated penetration which could change a table, violate security, and restore the table to its original configuration.

25. Insure that all system software documentation and stand-alone utility programs are properly locked up for physical security.

26. Insure that there are extraordinary controls in force either during a disaster or when new versions of system software are being tested because at that point the usual system software protective devices are not being utilized.

27. Determine whether someone is assigned to review the system logs on a periodic basis and look for illegal operator or user accesses and other security violations.

28. Do not allow application programmers to write and execute input/output programs directly. Always have them go through the data base management system, the recognized channel programs, and the like.

29. Consider storing sophisticated data that is utilized by system software in an encrypted fashion so if there were an unauthorized dump of either memory or disk it would be meaningless. Also, maintain a method of recording whenever there was a memory or disk dump. This can be used as an audit trail at a future time.

30. If a catastrophe occurs and portions of the system software are dumped, insure that these printouts are protected until the systems programmers are finished with them. Then they should be adequately disposed of (shredded or burned).

31. Whenever turning usage of a computer over to an outside third party, insure that the entire memory has been erased and that the system software has not been left behind.

32. Force the queuing system to fail and determine if it leaves sensitive information spread throughout the computer system.

33. Following a system catastrophe, insure that a terminal not logged on before the catastrophe cannot get logged on following the catastrophe without the full authentication sequence.

34. Should a communication circuit fail, insure that the communication software does not give that open port to the next terminal signing onto the system.

35. Insure that there are adequate maintenance and vendor support for all system software.

36. For microprogrammed software, review the procedures and protections to insure that the microcode has not been changed.

37. Insure that maintenance panels, CPUs, channels, control units, and any other devices are protected so spurious electrical signals cannot disorient the system software.

38. Whenever hardware monitors are utilized, insure that the people who design the experiments and attach the probes to the CPU are absolutely trustworthy. This also applies to software monitor programs.

39. Insure that vendors who perform any sort of maintenance to software are absolutely trustworthy; control their access and egress to the area.

40. Control the use of diagnostic testing programs.

41. Insure that the system software (operating system) is sufficiently sophisticated to keep track of the proportion of an authorized space allocation a program actually uses, and then that it efficiently and without compromising security erases only that portion of the memory, the disk, the tape, or the like.

42. Check the following loophole. To get efficient printer utilization, many systems spool their output (write output to a storage device for delayed printing). Most output spool programs have provisions so the operator may back up the pointer and restart the printout in event of a malfunction involving the printer, the ribbon, or the paper. Further, some programs allow the operator to request multiple originals even though this was not provided by the programmers. If an operator does either one of these options on a print file containing precious data, he or she can create a security violation. Does the operating system report to the master security console

that multiple printouts have been produced and must be accounted for? This type of loophole would also apply when spooled output is sent to a computer output microfilm (COM) device.

43. Insure that there is an adequate system software program change procedure with the appropriate authorization signatures for changing software.

44. Insure that there is a software program that controls the updating of both source and object code libraries and reports all changes, version numbers, saves prior versions, and the like.

45. Check address space. One of the most elementary ways to penetrate a system is to reference areas outside of the assigned memory space of the penetrators' (users') program. In this way, information can be read from or stored into the operating system software or other users' programs. Most systems have protective mechanisms against this basic form of penetration. These mechanisms might include hardware bounds registers used to check each memory reference dynamically to insure that the reference falls within the users' assigned memory area, hardware protection keys on memory blocks used to check each memory reference dynamically to insure that the user's key matched the key of the block being referenced, and hardware/software virtual memory mechanisms or dynamic address translation techniques used to isolate a user's address space from the address space of other users.

46. Check special instruction execution. Another form of penetration involves the execution of certain instructions, such as input/output instructions that would enable a penetrator (user) to read or write data to or from other users' files. Most systems protect against such penetration by designing these types of instructions as privileged and by permitting them to be executed only by the operating system.

47. Check privileged status acquisition. Another form of system software involves the acquisition of "privileged status" which permits the penetrator (user) to execute programs in operating system supervisor mode. Software should have protection devices to restrict the ability of a penetrator from getting into this privileged status mode.

48. Check system work area penetration. System work areas should be contained within the systems address space and thus be protected by the normal address space protection mechanisms; however, for a variety of reasons this is not always successful. Even the strict requirement that all work areas be maintained within the system's address space would not necessarily solve this problem because subroutine calling sequences or monitor calling sequences might be a path that would allow a penetrator (user) the ability to jump into someone else's program or work space area.

49. Check parameters. Whenever software does not adequately check parameters that are being passed between program modules, this could form a door through which a penetrator could enter. For example, a penetrator might succeed in gaining a forbidden service by passing a negative parameter value. Also, a new system software release may unexpectedly open up new holes in unanticipated places because the changes in one program area invalidate the checks existing in another area with regard to passing parameters.

50. Check preloaded program replacements. A penetration technique that could be utilized is the preloading of specialized system routines that have the same name as the system routine, thereby entering the bogus routine

in the system directory. During operation, a system, noting that the required routine is already loaded (bogus routine), would transfer control to the preloaded bogus routine rather than calling for its own copy from secondary storage. Therefore the penetrator has gained control and probably entered privileged supervisor status mode. Specialized system-routine directories should be kept in protected memory space or lockwords should be used.

51. Check file access. This category covers a multitude of possible penetrations all encompassing the accessing of files without the proper authorization. For example, a system backup or dump utility might make it possible for a penetrator to dump an entire disk pack if that utility ignored the protection keys of the individual files on the pack; a penetrator might programmatically test key combinations against a file having a short "keyword field" until he or she gained access; a computer operator might make an oversight in checking physical labels on a tape; and noncontrolled vendor utilities, and so on might allow a penetrator to gain access to the files.

52. Check residue information scavenging. This category involves accessing information left behind by other users. The information left behind may be stored on disk, tape, the computer's memory, etc. This type of penetration can be prevented by zeroing out the storage medium upon the release of the space by the original user.

53. Check Trojan Horse assaults. In this category the penetrator loads a properly authorized software program into the system but contained within that program is another improper or nonauthorized program. When the user calls the particular program, the system loads the entire program with the bogus routine and the bogus routine performs whatever it has been programmed to do. Check for embedded job control or embedded catalog or program calls as well as printing, on the console, new job calls.

54. Check remote access. Terminal access to a system introduces a new dimension to system software security problems. While these may not be directly related to software security, they do pose the problem that software has the potential of being attacked from a long distance away from the physical area where the software resides. A variety of possible penetration paths may exist so the software might check the various circuits to insure that they are the proper circuits and that the proper input/output transactions are being entered on these circuits; consider encryption of the data; limit the use of dial-up modems when they can be connected to highly sensitive and secure software systems; insure that when a communications circuit drops that there is an absolute physical dropping of the computer software so the next person dialing into the system will not be connected to the software or to another user's program; utilize passwords and various log-in codes, etc.

55. Check system overloading. Although overloading a system may occasionally result in errors or conditions that permit various types of security breaches, the primary impact of penetration in this category is to crash or otherwise render the system unavailable for service. If a penetrator were to cause a table or a queue to overflow, the system might be rendered inoperable; and during the recovery procedures it might be easier for a penetrator to damage the system. Insure that the software monitors and reports on "System Load."

56. Check synchronous/asynchronous mix-ups. Some computer systems employ synchronous processing techniques for certain functions in order to achieve greater efficiency. However, when the application of these techniques is extended to handle tasks that are asynchronous in nature the system

security can sometimes be penetrated. Consider an operating system that is paging fixed size pages to and from a fixed head disk. If the paging operations are scheduled on a slot or rotational position basis, they will exhibit many of the characteristics of a synchronous operation. Efficiency considerations may result in the system handling these operations on a synchronous rather than a completion interrupt basis. However, if on an input operation, the system transfers the data from its nonpaged system area to a user page after a fixed time interval, the penetrator can succeed in transferring data into a space no longer associated with himself by requesting input from an unexpectedly slower device. Depending upon the use to which the system might put such reassigned space, a variety of security violations might be possible.

57. Look for system bypass mechanisms. Many software systems have security bypass mechanisms to facilitate certain activities or functions. For example, there usually exists a "secret" monitor call for use by system programmers. This call will put a user program into supervisory state and therefore permit the execution of privileged instructions. The system should have a very positive method of controlling these security bypass mechanisms. Also, there are usually "hooks" and other features to facilitate system programs that are added locally. Usually these locally developed systems, programs, or bypasses are added without adequate protection and thereby render the system quite vulnerable.

58. Check penetration detection. Many systems do not provide appropriate penetration detection techniques. An example of these techniques might be an automatically triggered routine that would log a user off the system after three consecutive errors in logging-in. Another might be adequate reports to management with regard to certain attempted penetrations to the software or certain supervisory or utility subroutine calls. Another penetration detection device might be to develop appropriate audit trails and process these in real time so attempts in penetration could be thwarted before they succeeded. One proposed security measure in this area might be entrapment. This approach involves the inclusion of a number of very appealing looking holes or hooks in the operating system coupled with a very close monitoring of anyone who passes any program statements or data through these holes.

59. Check asynchronous suspensions. In some systems, security mechanisms break down or can be bypassed when execution is asynchronously interrupted. Thus, if a user hits the break key on a teletype to suspend execution of his time-sharing program (while he or she does some thinking or executes some other command) some files may be left in an open state and may be vulnerable to penetration. Similarly, in the event of a system crash, these files and programs may be vulnerable until a full recovery has been made. As with the system overloading discussion above, the penetrator can cause a system crash, or at least an operator-induced halt and restart, at a time of his or her choosing; thus he or she is in a good position to take advantage of such breaks in security.

60. Examine check-point/restart modifications. In this case, the penetrator takes a check-point of his or her program during its execution and subsequently operates upon the check-point file as if it were a regular data file. Since for restart purposes, the system must include all status and system registers in the check-point file, the penetrator can effectively change the contents of status or system registers (which could not otherwise be modified) by appropriately manipulating the check-point file. Then by restarting the program from the modified check-point file, the penetrator can execute

in a supervisory mode or whatever status desired. Log whenever a restart is executed or status/systems registers are dumped.

61. Check resource sharing. All too often attempts to offer resource sharing have resulted in a penetrator being able to access (share) a program without authorization or to insert a program that someone may share unsuspectingly. The sharing of mechanisms frequently results in breakdowns relating to the read and/or write access to various directories; therefore, all directories and user files should have lockwords.

62. Check intelligence gathering. In this category the penetrator seeks to infer private information by using an appropriate combination of legitimate facilities or by taking advantage of particular characteristics of other users' programs. For example, scanning a directory is not generally viewed as a security violation since no data contained within a file is revealed by this action. Yet, by learning the size of a particular file, the penetrator may be able to infer confidential information (file size may be directly related to the number of account records being maintained). All directories should be lockword protected.

63. Check operator circumvention. Any operating systems depend upon the operator to perform a variety of security functions. Thus the operator may be the only security mechanism for checking the validity of requested tape mounts. Insure that any operator circumventions of various security requirements (either automated or manual) are duly logged.

64. Check user laxity. Regardless of the sophistication of system software protection mechanisms, user laxity can result in their circumvention. When mechanisms become difficult to use or remember, users tend to ignore or avoid them. A prime example of this problem involves passwords.

65. Check removal or addition of software code. However achieved, the removal or addition of code from the software could pose a security threat. The use of a check-sum bit count with regard to sensitive software packages might be an appropriate measure to insure against unauthorized program changes.

66. Look for exploitable logic errors. In any major software system there are, at any point in time, some "bugs" or errors. Some of these may be documented but not yet corrected. A logic error may be exploited by a penetrator in order to compromise the integrity of the software. Logic errors should be evaluated with regard to their potential security risk if they must remain uncorrected for any period of time.

67. Check software generation options. Vendor software packages usually contain many options that can be called upon when generating the software system. All the security options must be reviewed and evaluated and a positive decision made whenever one of them is not to be used to its fullest extent. Also, any options that are left to the default state should be tested. In other words, the default mechanism should be tested in order to insure that it is operating correctly and not branching to some protected or restricted area of memory or someone else's program space.

68. Check interrupt handling. During the handling of interrupt, various parameters are stored. Insure that these parameters are stored in protected memory space, protected registers, or other protected areas.